MOUNT NEBO. AN ARCHAEOLOGICAL SURVEY OF THE REGION

MOUNT NEBO
An Archaeological Survey of the Region
Vol. I The Palaeolithic and the Neolithic Periods
Proceedings of the Danish Institute in Damascus, 8
© The authors 2013
Layout and typesetting Carmelo Pappalardo
Cover photo: By Peder Mortensen. View towards SW from a small Middle Palaeolithic open-air site
(*MN 409*) on the northern side of Wadi Kanisah. September 1993.
Printed by Ferrari srl, Milano
ISBN 978 87 7124 078 8

Printed in Italy 2013

Aarhus University Press
Langelandsgade 177
DK-8200 Aarhus N
www.unipress.dk

Whiate Cross Mills
Hightown, Lancaster, LA1 4XS
United Kingdom
www.gazellebooks.co.uk

ISD
70 Enterprise Drive
Bristol, CT 06010
USA

Published with the financial support from
The Danish Palestine Foundation

During the survey at Mount Nebo
all sites and monuments were measured and described in the field
by Ingolf Thuesen and Inge Demant Mortensen;
they were photographed by Peder Mortensen

Artefacts were drawn
by Peder Mortensen and Louise Hilmar,
maps by Ingolf Thuesen and Tim Skuldbøl

MOUNT NEBO. AN ARCHAEOLOGICAL SURVEY OF THE REGION

VOL. I
The Palaeolithic and the Neolithic Periods

Peder Mortensen
Ingolf Thuesen and Inge Demant Mortensen

Proceedings of the Danish Institute in Damascus, 8

❱ Michele Piccirillo with Peder Mortensen at Mount Nebo, Maj 2007.

In memory of fr. Michele Piccirillo (1944 – 2008)
an eminent scholar and a close friend

⟩ CONTENTS ⟨

) ILLUSTRATIONS (

⟩ PREFACE ⟨

The connection between Danish archaeologists and the Franciscan Archaeological Institute at Mount Nebo was first established in 1991. During this year a large exhibition of Widad Kawar's collection of women's costumes from Palestine and Jordan was shown in Denmark at the Moesgaard Museum near Aarhus together with an important selection of Byzantine mosaics from chapels and churches in Jordan.[1] Most of these mosaics had been excavated by the Franciscan Archaeological Institute at Mount Nebo under the direction of fr. Michele Piccirillo, the distinguished explorer of the mosaics of Jordan, to the memory of whom this volume is dedicated.

During his visit to Denmark in 1991 Michele Piccirillo described the changes and the serious destruction of archaeological sites which during these years took place in the region around Mount Nebo.

In conversations with Piccirillo he mentioned that he wished to create a kind of archaeological park where a number of exceptional archaeological and historical monuments within the range of Mount Nebo could be registered, protected and, hopefully, in the future could be included among the world heritage sites by UNESCO.[2] As a result of these initial discussions, it was decided – in collaboration with a group of Danish archaeologists – to carry out an intensive survey in order to locate, describe and map the archaeological sites, which still remained around Mount Nebo.

The authors wish to thank the Danish Palestine Foundation for its generous support to this project and the Franciscan Archaeological Institute at Mount Nebo for help and hospitality to such an extent that we happily felt that at Mount Nebo we were at home, treated as "members of the family". Finally we wish to express our gratitude to fr. Carmelo Pappalardo, not only for his friendship and his highly qualified participation in the survey, but also for his professional advice and help towards getting this volume edited and printed.

....

[1] Piccirillo 1991: 30 ff.
[2] Piccirillo and Palumbo 1993; Sabelli and Dinelli 1998.

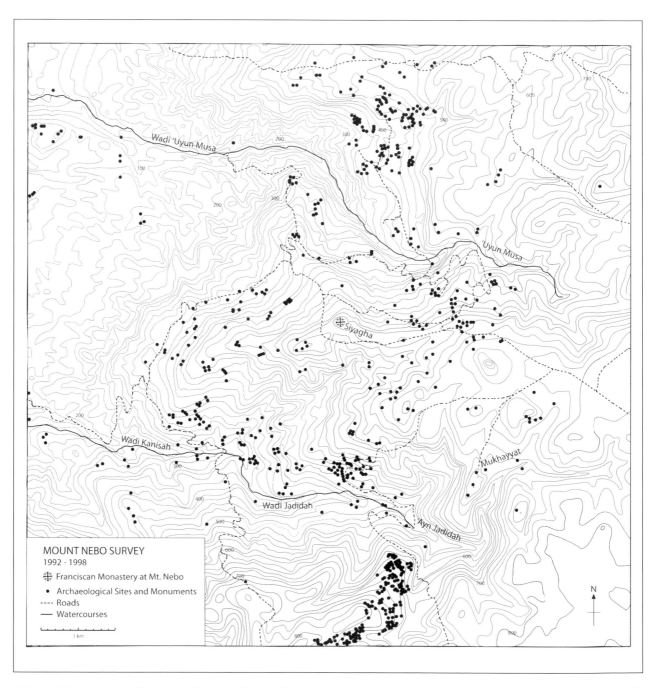

》Fɪɢ. 1 Map showing the area of Mount Nebo. The sites and monuments registered during the survey 1992-1998 are indicated by dots.

) INTRODUCTION (

The Franciscan Monastery at Mount Nebo, including the Archaeological Institute, is situated at Siyagha, c. 7 km northwest of Madaba, at an elevation of approximately 695 metres above sea level (*Fig. 1*). Siyagha is surrounded by a rolling landscape consisting of eroded sand and limestone deposits forming the western flanks of the Jordanian Highlands. It continues towards east as a plateau where the highest point east of Khirbat al-Mukhayyat reaches a height of 827 metres. Further east it runs into the Madaba Plain. The main topographical features in the region are the two major valleys, south and north of Siyagha: to the south Wadi Jadidah continuing into Wadi Kanisah and to the north Wadi 'Uyun Musa. Nowadays, the irrigated valleys both make their way towards west from the springs of 'Ayn Jadidah and 'Uyun Musa, down into the Jordanian Rift Valley (*Figs. 2-6*).

During the Pleistocene and Holocene periods the topography of the Mount Nebo region has been altered by erosion which still today seems to be an active factor in the transformation of the landscape (*Fig. 7*). Like other wadies along the Western Highlands,[3] the terraces and slopes of the two valleys along either side of Mount Nebo reflect a sequence of ruptures and incisions, followed by periods of alluvial filling and of new incisions caused by climatic fluctuations throughout the Pleistocene and Holocene periods. Here geomorphological changes have also affected the depositional history of the archaeological remains. Many artefacts, particularly those of Pleistocene date, are found secondarily deposited in soils removed from their original position by natural agents, and Palaeolithic open-air sites, which may have been covered by layers of later sediments, re-appear *in situ* after having been exposed to alluvial or aeolian erosion (*Fig. 8*). In some areas the original rock surface has been exposed (*Figs. 9-10*), probably resulting from extensive land-use and deforestation in Byzantine and Early Islamic times.[4] Remains of stone-built walls and terraces, which most probably can be related to these periods, seem to confirm the impression of intensive agricultural activities in the 5th-7th centuries (*Figs. 11-12*).

The region is rich in ancient sites and monuments, first described by Félicien De Saulcy in 1865 after his visit to Jordan in 1863 and by Le Duc de Luynes, who visited Siyagha in 1864.[5] The admirable work of one of the later 19th century pioneers has been of special relevance for us: during his exploration of Eastern Palestine in the

---

[3] Cf. Macumber 2008: 24-29.

[4] On the effects of land-use and deforestation in the Late Classical and Early Islamic periods see Bintliff 2002: 417 ff., Butzer 2005: 1773 ff., and Walmsley 2007: 112 and 135 ff.

[5] De Saulcy 1865, I: 289-296 and Luynes 1874: 148-154. For an extensive account on the early exploration of Mount Nebo see Piccirillo and Alliata 1998:13-51.

1880's Colonel C. R. Conder succeeded in making a thorough mapping and drawing of many monuments in the area around Mount Nebo, including the dolmens south of Siyagha.[6] More than a hundred years later his publication was of great help, when our team revisited the megalithic monuments he had described (*Figs. 13-14*). Since then many prehistoric and classical sites and monuments have been described and excavated in the area,[7] but by far the most remarkable investigations were carried out since 1933 at Siyagha, Khirbat al-Mukhayyat and at a number of other important archaeological sites by members of the Studium Biblicum Franciscanum.[8] The research was interrupted by the Arab-Israeli war in 1967, when Siyagha was declared a military zone. But in 1976 the work was resumed in full scale by the Franciscan Archaeological Institute at Mount Nebo, established under the direction of Michele Piccirillo. After his untimely death in 2008, the work has been carried on by some of his close collaborators under the leadership of Carmelo Pappalardo, who during two decades, always close at hand, followed and assisted Michele Piccirillo in his research.

Although the bottom of the two wadies and part of the plateau east of Siyagha was cultivated, most of the land lay waste and was used primarily by bedouins, who in this landscape would find enough food for their sheep and goats. In recent time, however, several new settlements and roads were constructed and cultivation was intensified, especially by the building of stone-lined agricultural terraces which were irrigated by way of pumps from small artificial water reservoirs. These activities caused the destruction of many archaeological sites: some were disturbed or simply removed by bulldozers, others were covered by new fertile soil taken from other regions, and in many cases large stones from megalithic monuments were split and used as material for the building of fences or stone walls along new agricultural terraces (*Figs. 15-17* and *91-92*). These activities were accompanied by an increasing number of illicit excavations and destruction of ancient burials, in particular dolmens and megalithic circular tombs (*Figs. 18-22*).

....

[6] Conder 1885: 106-155 and 1889: 98-101 and 254-275. Colonel Conder's reconnaissance of Eastern Palestine in 1881 was carried out at a time, when the Ottoman government had categorically refused any kind of foreign exploration in the region. In his subsequent publication Conder vividly describes the conditions under which he had to work. We quote from his report (Conder 1885): "*The more quietly we set to work, the more likely we should be to excite suspicion, and yet the only hope of doing anything at all lay in escaping for a time the vigilance of the Government*" (107). "*[…] when we remember the lamentable fate of Professor Palmer and his companions, betrayed by an Arab Shaikh, and butchered in the heart of the desert by Bedawin set on probably by the creatures of the rebel Egyptian Government, it will, I think, be allowed that our mission was pushed to the utmost limits […]. Had a single member lost his life on that expedition, I should have had a heavy burden on my conscience for having let him in to danger; and it is not always when things appear to be going smoothly, and Arabs are obsequious and Governors apparently asleep, that a small party of explorers is really most safe*" (109-110). "*Thus our presence was certain to be discovered sooner or later, through the jealousy of some Government creature among the Bedawin […]* (but) *although discovered four weeks after crossing* (the Jordan River), *we did not finally leave Moab until the 29th of October, and during this period of eleven weeks we surveyed in all nearly 500 square miles, discovered 700 rude stone monuments, and obtained a volume of notes, plans, and drawings, while Lieutenant Mantell took forty photographs*" (122).

[7] Ripamonti 1963; Saller 1966; Stockton 1967; Palumbo 1998; Benedettucci 1998.

[8] The excavations and restorations of Byzantine churches, chapels and other buildings carried out by the Franciscan archaeologists are described by Saller 1941; Saller and Bagatti 1949; Schneider 1950, and in particular by Piccirillo and Alliata 1998. See also the annual reports on archaeological investigations carried out under the auspices of the Archaeological Institute at Mount Nebo, published in Jerusalem in the *Liber Annuus* (Studium Biblicum Franciscanum).

During six seasons (1992-1998) an intensive survey of the Mount Nebo region was accomplished under the auspices of the Franciscan Archaeological Institute at Mount Nebo and the Danish Palestine Foundation. It was followed by a brief reconnaissance in 2008. The survey was carried out in the field by a small group of archaeologists, directed by Peder Mortensen and including Inge Demant Mortensen (1992-1995, 1997-1998 and 2008), Niels H. Andersen (1992), Ingolf Thuesen (1993-1995, 1997-1998 and 2008), and Francesco Benedettucci (1994-1995 and 1997-1998). The group was occasionally joined by Michele Piccirillo and by Carmelo Pappalardo from the Franciscan Archaeological Institute.[9] Subsequently, during the years 2000-2001 and 2003-2005 excavations were carried out at a site called "Conder's Circle" near 'Ayn Jadidah,[10] an enigmatical monument, the date of which seems to range from the Late Chalcolithic into the Early Bronze Age I period (*Fig. 23*).

Centered around Siyagha, the survey covered an area of approximately 35 square kilometres, within the region, which in the UTM system is defined by the coordinates North 3.514.000 – 3.522.000, East 754.000 – 762.000.[11] The entire region, varying in elevation from -100 to +800 metres, was subdivided into topographically defined sub-areas including the heights and the rolling hills, the wadi systems, terraces and plateaus, and the bare flat country east of the wadies. The selected sub-areas were systematically surveyed by members of the expedition walking across the fields and slopes. There were, however, areas or locations which were inaccessible for the archaeologists involved in the project. This included e.g. a mine field from the Arab-Israeli war on the slopes west of Siyagha and a few almost vertical formations along the southern side of Wadi Kanisah and at the eastern end of Wadi Jadidah.

In late August, September and October, when our field work was carried out, the landscape appeared barren and burnt after the dry summer months. This situation facilitated the survey and brought out more clearly surface scatters of flints and potsherds and the traces of walls and other ancient structures. Exceptions were the irrigated plantations, which might be covered with a dense vegetation of fruit trees and vegetables or a carpet of weeds and grass. Another obstacle was new settlements, gardens or plots of land surrounded by barbed wire in order to keep sheep and goats out. During the survey, however, we were able to cover most of these "closed" areas prior to cultivation, or with the kind permission of the landowners.

....

[9] Mortensen 1992, 1996 and 2009; Thuesen 2004; Mortensen and Thuesen 2007.

[10] Mortensen 2002, 2005; Mortensen and Thuesen 2007; Thuesen 2009.

[11] All sites are recorded by UTM coordinates in agreement with the Jordanian Antiquities Database and Information System (JADIS: cf. Palumbo 1994). British maps of the region were used as base maps, supplemented by air photos recorded in 1972. Several methods were used in the field and in camp to obtain as precisely as possible the coordinates for each site. The simplest mapping method involved identifying the sites on air photos, which was done on location. This allowed for a transfer to a map with the UTM grid and was a procedure that could be carried out in most cases. As an independent check on the position of a site, compass readings were carried out systematically to a fixed point in the landscape. For example there is visual contact with the large cross in front of the Memorial of Moses at Siyagha from most positions within the survey. In 1994 the Geographical Position System (GPS) was introduced, in which UTM coordinates are determined with the use of satellites. With a differential correction from a base station at ACOR in Amman it was now possible to determine the UTM coordinates with a precision of < 5 metres, which was far more accurate than any other method, based on the available maps, allowed.

748 single objects, sites and monuments – in time ranging from the Lower Palaeolithic to the Late Ottoman periods – were located. As soon as a feature or a scatter of artefacts was recognized, the site was successively given an identification number: **MN 1-748**. Surface scatters of artefacts were sampled, and the size of the scatter was estimated. Diagnostic finds were kept for drawing and description back in the laboratory. Visible monuments, such as tombs, were photographed, measured and described in the field (*Figs. 24-25*), and in case there were associated artefacts any diagnostic items were collected. These informations were later entered into a database (FileMaker) that contains all available records from the survey: the position of the sites, site characteristics, photos, drawings, maps, and a list of objects collected at the site during the survey.

Our attention was primarily concentrated on the large number of megalithic monuments in the Mount Nebo area: 194 dolmens, 41 lines of stones and menhirs, and 316 circular megalithic tombs. Together with other finds from the Chalcolithic, Bronze- and Iron Ages, and from the Persian, Hellenistic, Roman, Byzantine and Islamic periods they will be described in two successive publications.

This volume, however, is dedicated to the description of 79 locations and single finds, which can be attributed to the Stone Age. In our presentation the material has been divided into four chronological groupings, covering the Lower, Middle, Upper–Epipalaeolithic, and the Neolithic periods. As it will appear in the following chapters, a more fine-meshed division of the material within the individual periods is sometimes possible. It is also worth mentioning that several assemblages reflect a situation, where a site has been occupied during more than one period,[12] in which case the site is indicated several times at the relevant chronological maps. In our description of the assemblages and at the distribution maps we have chosen to differentiate between three categories of collections: *single finds*, *scatters of finds,* usually comprising less than 30 objects, and *concentrations of finds* which seem to represent an actual occupation of the locality within a restricted area. In connection with the description of these categories only locations and artefacts relating to concentrations of finds are illustrated in this volume by photographs and drawings.

Finally, it is important to emphasize, that the aim in this context was limited to making a chronological identification of the assemblages and their distribution in the landscape, based on diagnostic artifacts, such as for example Acheulean handaxes, Levallois- and Mousterian points, Neolithic arrowheads, bipolar blade cores, and pottery. Therefore we did not in the field make any attempt to collect *all* objects or to make a systematic study of their distribution within a site. With this in mind, and using a method by which a very limited collection of artefacts were removed from the individual locations, it should be possible in the future to identify the sites where enough material has been left to carry out further systematic investigations and possibly excavations in case this would seem to be appropriate.

---

[12] Middle Palaeolithic concentrations of finds were associated with scatters of Epipalaeolithic artefacts at two locations (**MN 41** and **MN 581**). Scatters of Middle Palaeolithic artefacts were found at three locations (**MN 72, MN 589,** and **MN 647**). Scatters of Middle Palaeolithic and PPNB-flints were found at **MN 536**. A scatter of Middle Palaeolithic finds was associated with a concentration of Epipalaeolithic flints (**MN 672**), scatters of Middle Palaeolithic and Epipalaeolithic artefacts were found with a concentration of PPNB-flints (**MN 673**), and a concentration of Epipalaeolithic finds was associated with a scatter of PPNB-flints (**MN 574**).

❱ Fɪɢ. 2 A view towards south, across Wadi Musa towards Siyagha with the Franciscan Monastery at Mount Nebo on top of the hill in the background. September 1993.

⟩ FIG. 3 The western section of Wadi Musa with an Epipalaeolithic site (**MN 455**) on top of the central plateau in the middle, seen towards east. September 1995.

❭ FIG. 4 Track leading down to 'Ayn Jadidah with an irrigated garden in the bottom of the valley to the left. September 1994.

⟩ Fɪɢ. 5 A view across Wadi Jadidah showing a section of heavy alluvial formations along the southern side of the valley. September 1994.

❭ FIG. 6 The western end of Wadi Kanisah with a view towards north and with a stone-covered burial mound (**MN 431**) in front of the picture. September 1994.

❭ FIG. 15 A small Pre-Pottery Neolithic site (**MN 425**), being destroyed by recent building activities. September 2008.

❭ FIG. 16 Construction of stone-lined terraces in a garden south-east of Siyagha. September 1998.

❱ Fɪɢ. 17 Modern dirt-tracks cutting through a group of megalithic tombs (**MN 321-324**).October 1992.

❭ Fig. 18 Recently plundered megalithic tomb (**MN 412**) south of Wadi Kanisah. September 1993.

❯ Fɪɢ. 19 A young bedouin happily playing his flute on top of a recently plundered tomb (**MN 80**). September 1993.

❯ FIG. 24   Ingolf Thuesen and Inge Demant Mortensen measuring and describing a megalithic tomb, encircled by two lines of large, standing ashlars (**MN 13**). September 1993.

❭ Fɪɢ. 25 Inge Demant Mortensen and Niels H. Andersen measuring two dolmens (**MN 141-142**) at the plateau south of 'Ayn Jadidah. September 1992.

❱ Fɪɢ. 27 View towards the Lower Palaeolithic site **MN 575**, situated at the saddle-shaped plateau on top of a hill on the southern side of Wadi Hesban. September 1997.

❭ FIG. 28 View towards east across the saddle-shaped plateau with the Lower Palaeolithic site **MN 575**. In the foreground Michele Piccirillo. September 1998.

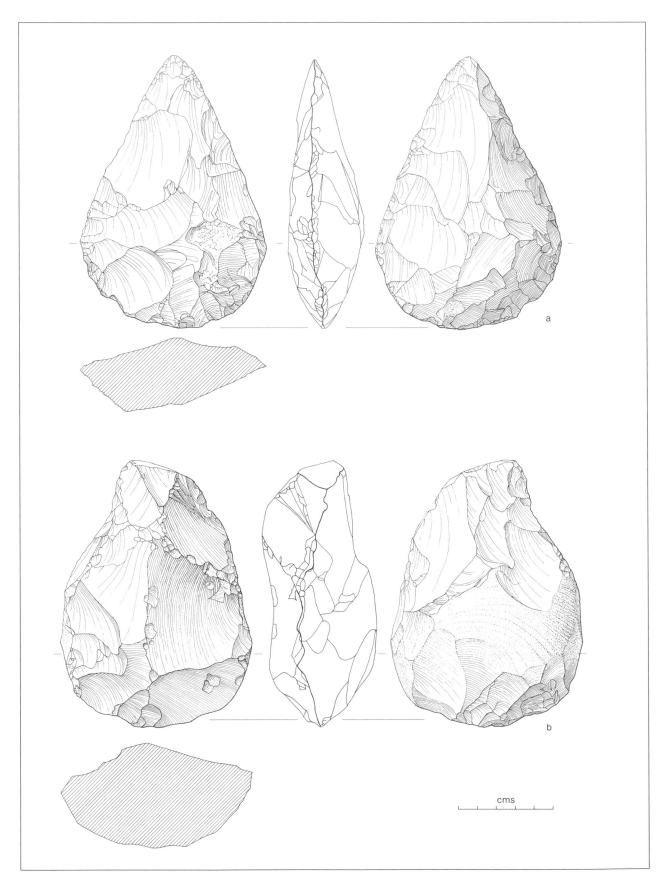

▶ Fig. 29 Lower Palaeolithic handaxes from **MN 575**.

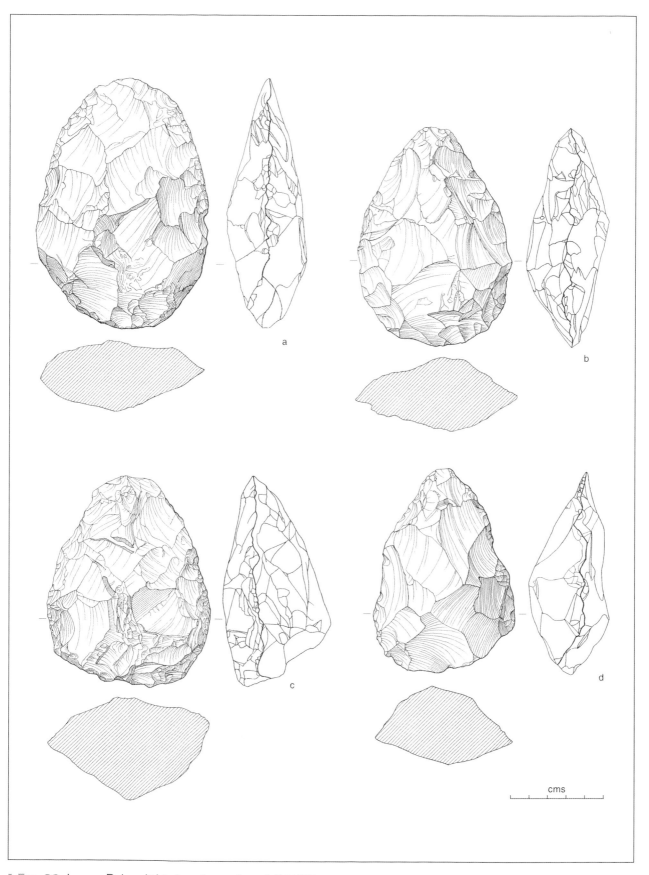

) FIG. 30 Lower Palaeolithic handaxes from **MN 575**.

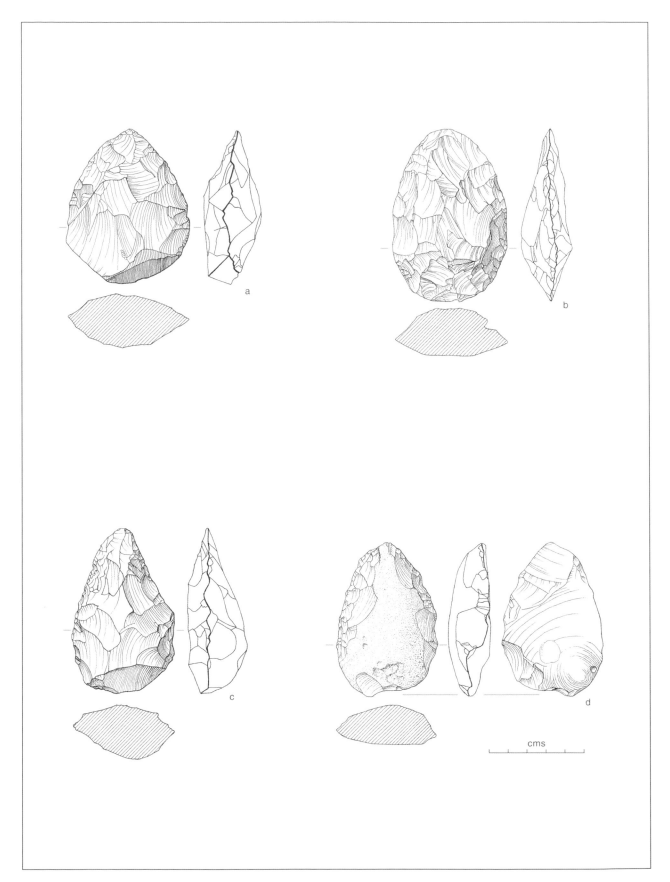

❱ Fig. 31 Lower Palaeolithic handaxes from **MN 575**.

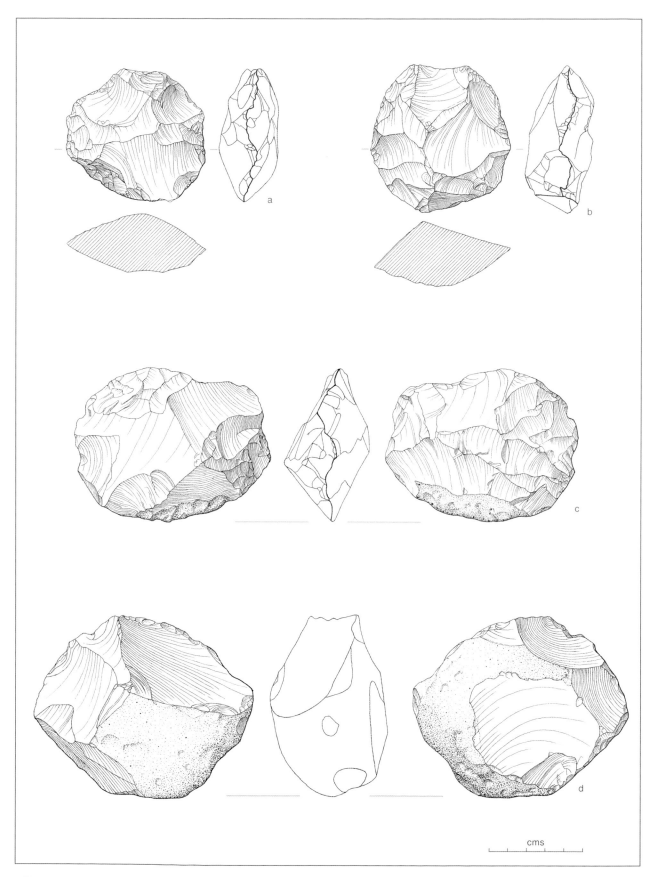

) FIG. 32 Lower Palaeolithic artefacts from **MN 575**: discos-shaped bifaces (**a-b**) and chopping-tools (**c-d**).

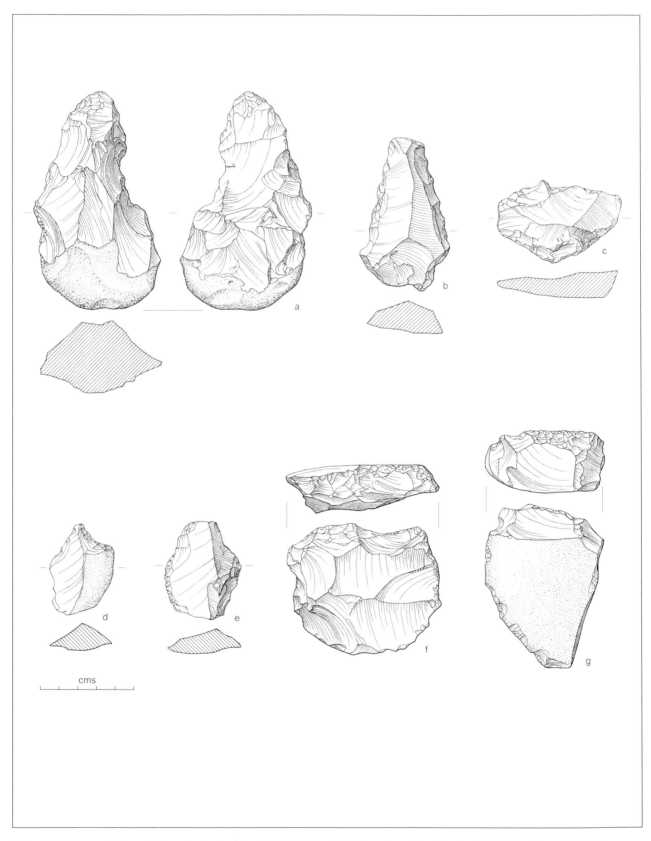

❱ Fɪɢ. 33 Lower Palaeolithic artefacts from **MN 575**: pick (**a**), point, the tip of which is broken off (**b**), borers (**c-d**), side-scraper (**e**), end-scraper made on the lower part of a broken handaxe (**f**), and an end-scraper made on a core fragment (**g**).

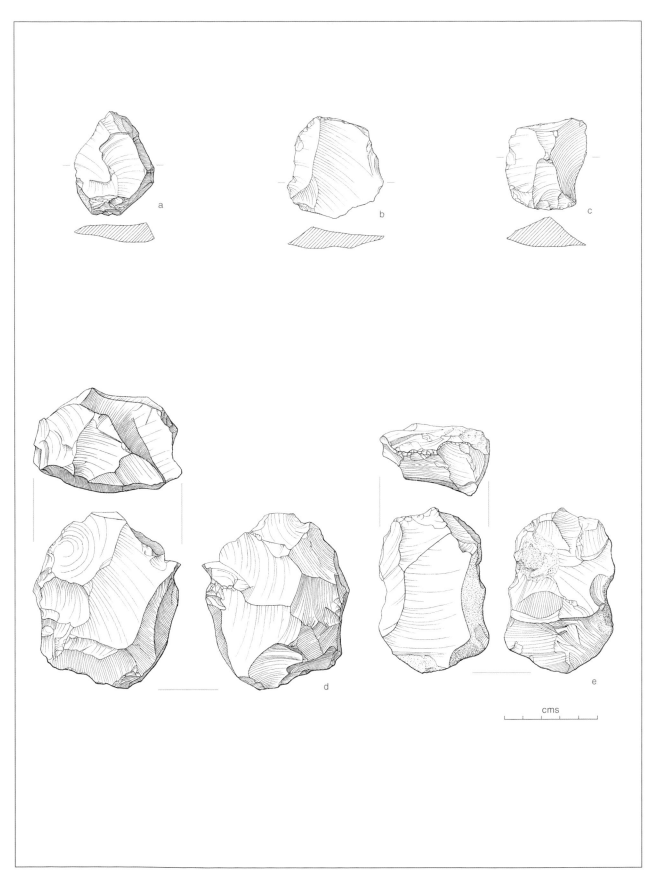

) FIG. 34 Lower Palaeolithic artefacts from **MN 575**: flakes (**a-c**) and flake-cores (**d-e**).

❱ FIG. 35 View towards north-east across the Lower Palaeolithic site **MN 697**. September 2008.

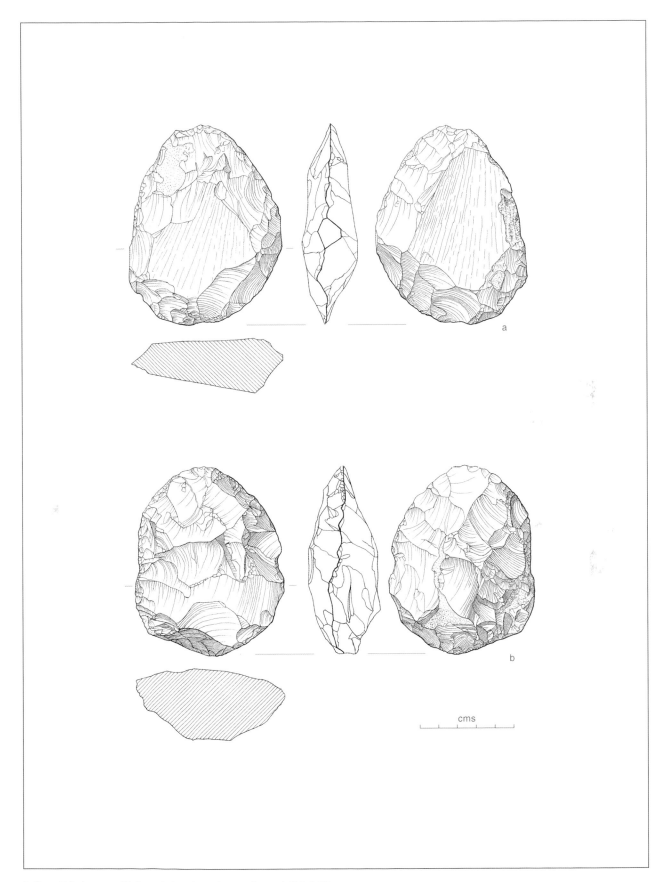

❱ Fig. 36 Lower Palaeolithic handaxes from **MN 697**.

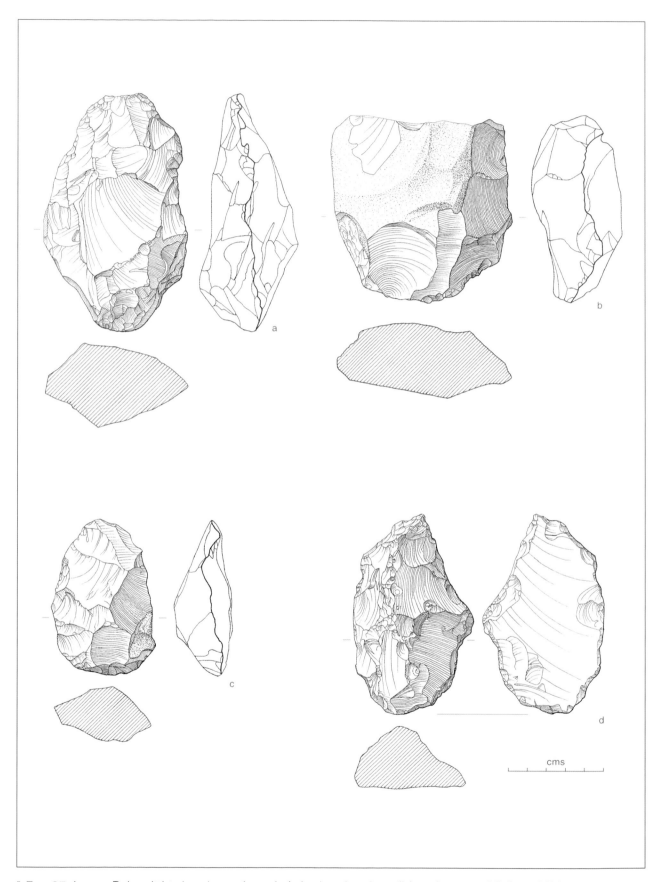

❱ FIG. 37 Lower Palaeolithic handaxes (**a** and **c**), broken handaxe (**b**) and a point (**d**) from **MN 697**.

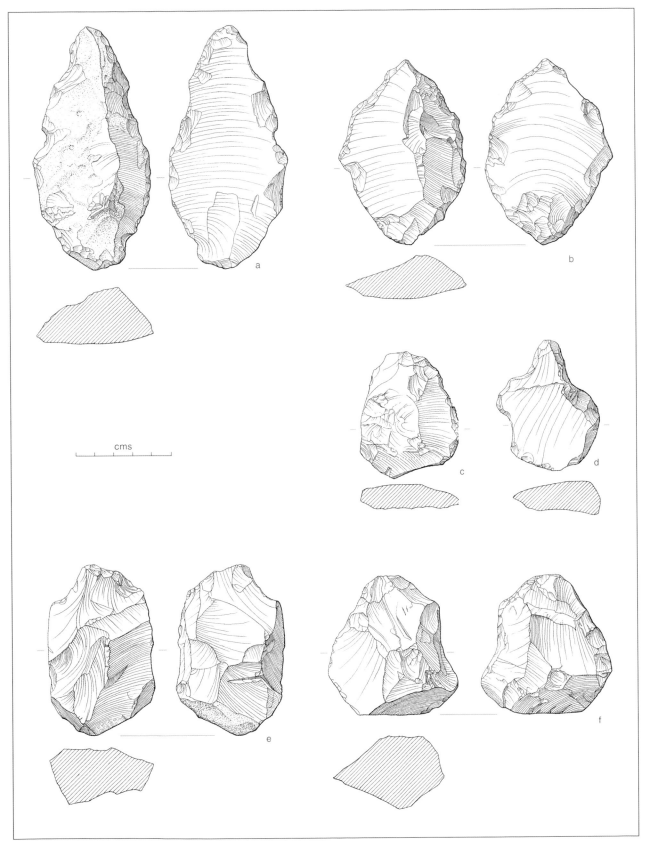

cms

) FIG. 38 Lower Palaeolithic artefacts from **MN 697**: pick (**a**), point (**b**), side-scraper (**c**), borer (**d**), and two flake cores (**e-f**).

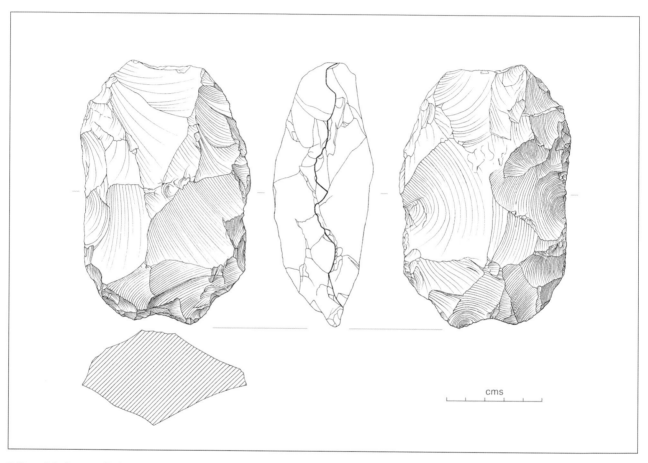

❱ Fɪɢ. 39 Lower Palaeolithic cleaver: **MN 358**.

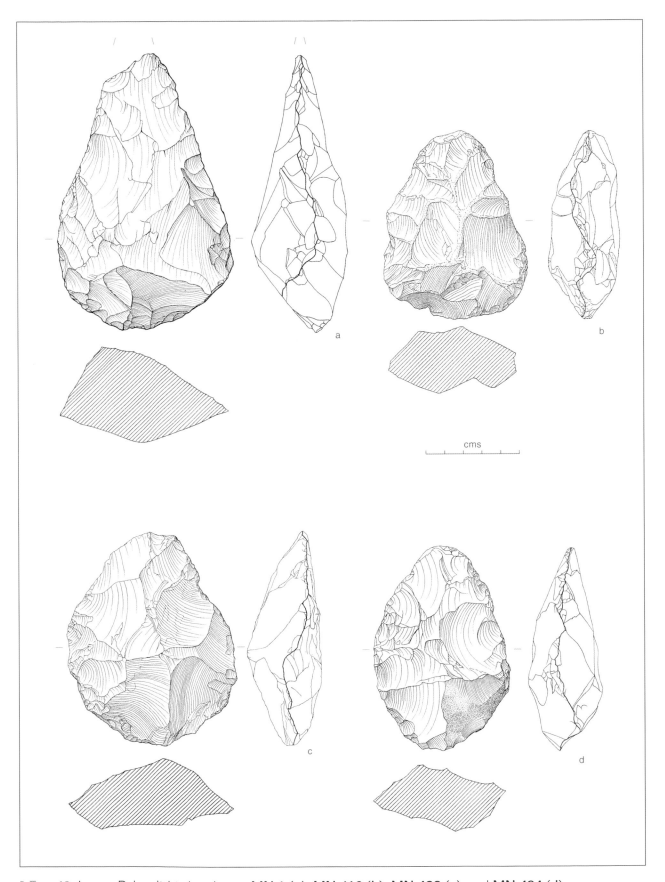

cms

❯ FIG. 40 Lower Palaeolithic handaxes: **MN 1 (a)**, **MN 419 (b)**, **MN 433 (c)**, and **MN 484 (d)**.

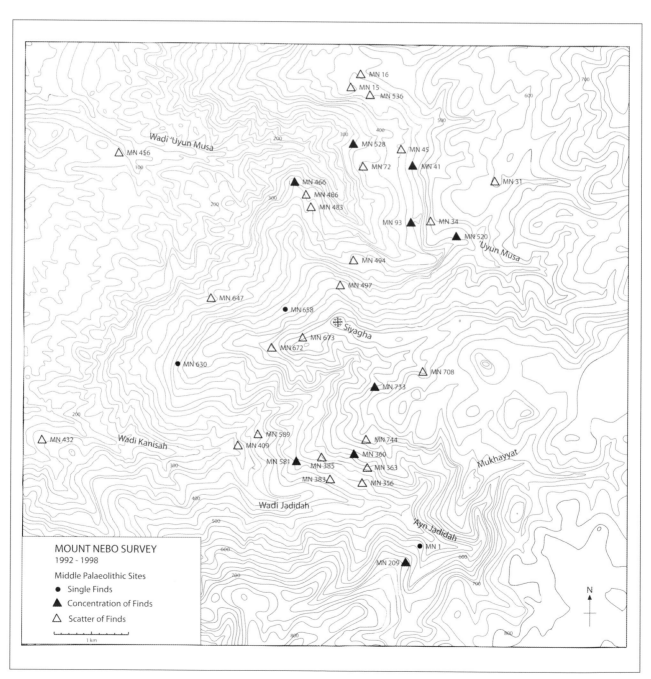

FIG. 41 Map showing the distribution of Middle Palaeolithic sites and single finds.

⟩ THE MIDDLE PALAEOLITHIC PERIOD ⟨

At a number of Middle Palaeolithic sites an additional element of Upper– Epipalaeolithic flints occurs: **MN 41**, **MN 72**, **MN 581**, **MN 589**, **MN 647**, **MN 672** and **MN 630**; at **MN 673** both Upper– Epipalaeolithic and a major dominance of PPNB flints were discovered, and at **MN 536** both Middle Palaeolithic and PPNB flints were found.

Our distinction between flints from various periods occurring at one site is primarily based on typological criteria.

Furthermore, it is conspicuous that different sources of raw material seem to have been in use during the Palaeolithic and Neolithic periods in the Mount Nebo region.

More than 90% of the Middle Palaeolithic artefacts were made from a very light brown tabular flint covered by a white or yellowish white patina. Outcrops of this type of flint occur e.g. at the important Middle Palaeolithic site **MN 360** (*Figs. 8 and 46-47*).

In contrast to the Middle Palaeolithic, a majority of the Upper– Epipalaeolithic artefacts were made of a grey to greyish-brown, unpatinated flint, possibly in most cases of nodular origin (as for example *Fig. 75 m*).

The PPNB artefacts were produced from an excellent pink-reddish brown flint, large nodules of which were located on a hill southwest of Siyagha (**MN 674**, *Fig. 89*).

Like the Middle Palaeolithic sites from the Jordanian Western Highland and the Central Plateau, the inventory of the Middle Palaeolithic sites from Mount Nebo falls within the Levantine Levallois-Mousterian tradition.

Characteristic of our collections from this period is a strong element of cores with a prepared platform, as for example Levallois cores (*Figs. 42 e, 45 f, and 58 m-n*), small broad-based Levallois and Mousterian points (*Figs. 42 a, 45 a-c, 48 a-c, 52 a-b, and 58 a-b*), Levallois flakes, and tools made from Levallois cores and flakes (*Figs. 42 f, 44 c, 48 f-g, 49 a, and 58 e and h-i*).

Small discos-shaped bifaces and handaxes (*Figs. 42 h, 44 g, 45 h, 50 b, and 54 a-b*) occur at several of the Middle Palaeolithic sites. They might be interpreted as Lower Palaeolithic leftovers, but since they are made of the same kind of flint as the Mousterian tools, it is more likely that they represent a bifacial technology, elements of which are still visible at many Middle Palaeolithic occupations in the Levant.[16]

As at most of the Mousterian assemblages from nearby Wadi al-Koum and Wadi Zarqa' Ma'in in the western part of the Madaba Plateau and some sites from the Wadi Hasa region in the south, the composition of the lithic collections from Mount Nebo seems to suggest a date within the later part of the Levantine Levallois-Mousterian tradition, as represented at Tabun B.[17]

If this tentative chronological framework is correct, it leaves a considerable gap between the exploitation of the region by *homo erectus* in the Upper Achaeulean period (c. 250,000-150,000 years bp) and the arrival in the Mount Nebo region

---

[16] Cf. e.g. Bisson *et al*. 2007: 182.
[17] Cf. Bar-Yosef 1998: 44 ff.; Bisson *et al*. 2007: 179 ff.; Henry 2007: 172 ff.; Olszewski 2008: 43.

of Neanderthals represented by a late Levallois-Mousterian tradition (Tabun B) c. 70,000 years bp.[18]

On the distribution of Middle Palaeolithic sites, it should be noted, that three concentrations of flint were located in the vicinity of 'Ayn Jadidah at hills and terraces 500 – 640 metres above sea level (**MN 209**, **MN 360**, and **MN 581**). Five concentrations were found 380 – 550 metres above sea level within a radius of c. 1 km along the eastern and northeastern side of Wadi Musa, not far from the present spring (**MN 41**, **MN 93**, **MN 466**, **MN 520**, and **MN 528**), and one concentration appeared on a sloping hillside c. 2 km north of Wadi Jadidah, 753 metres above sea level (**MN 733**).

The concentrations of finds are thus limited to two clusters near 'Ayn Jadidah and along the inner, northeastern side of Wadi 'Uyun Musa. These clusters are located on slopes and terraces near natural sources of water. In contrast to this pattern, the scatters of finds and single finds are widely distributed within the region (cf. the distribution map *Fig. 41*).

It should be noted in this connection that although we have found a few handaxes and several Middle Palaeolithic artefacts, such as Mousterian and Levallois points near caves and shelters, we have not been able to discover any Lower or Middle Palaeolithic occupation in or at the caves in the Mount Nebo region.[19] One reason may be that most of the caves are facing north, a direction which did not seem attractive for the Near Eastern Neanderthals for permanent or even seasonal settlement.

The concentrations of artefacts are all rather small, with an extension ranging from c. 10 x 20 metres to c. 50 x 60 metres, but since hardly any of the

locations have escaped being affected by alluvial or aeolian erosion, very little can be said about the original surface of the sites. One exception seems to be **MN 360** where a concentration of flints was found on a plateau above the northern side of Wadi Jadidah. The site may have been covered by later deposits of sand and gravel, but as it appears now, most of the original surface of the occupation has been re-exposed by wind erosion (*Figs. 8 and 46-47*). A natural outcrop of tabular flint cuts the site diagonally, and the composition of artefacts, including very few tools, but a predominance of primary and secondary raw materials (cores, core fragments, flakes, and lumps of tabular flint still *in situ*) suggests that the site may have functioned as a workshop for the production of tools.

The Middle Palaeolithic sites in the Mount Nebo region, situated in the wadies at hills and terraces near water, might possibly fit into a pattern of transhumance as described by Donald O. Henry (2007:171 ff.). He suggests that "[...] *Levantine Moustrian sites dated to some 50 – 70,000 years ago and situated from near sea-level in the Rift Valley to 1,600 m on the Ma'an Plateau [...] might reflect a strategy with long term winter encampments at lower elevations and warm season camps at high elevations [...] in which groups dispersed into small social units that were sustained through local, opportunistic provisioning within a site's catchment*".

Situated between 380 and 753 metres above sea level, the concentrations of Levallois-Mousterian artefacts in the Mount Nebo region might in this case be interpreted as representing small seasonal campsites used temporarily by minor groups of hunter-gatherers on the move between their win-

---

[18] There seems to be a general agreement in considering the Levallois-Mousterian tradition in the Levant as an exponent of the Neanderthals (Akazawa, Aoki and Bar-Yosef 1998; Finleyson 2004). It is notable in this context that at Dederiyeh in northern Syria two fragmentary skeletons of Neanderthals were found in a Tabun B-phase context at Dederiyeh (Muhesen 2004: 40 ff.). Usually the final examples of the Tabun B-phase of the Levantine Levallois-Mousterian are dated around 47,000 years bp., but as noted by Richter *et al.* (2001: 46): "*The new TL age estimate of the Late Middle Palaeolithic of 33.3 + -2.3 ka at Jefr al-Ajla (at the Syrian desert plateau) stress the occurrence of a considerable overlap of Middle and Upper Palaeolithic in the Levant*".

[19] During a survey of the Madaba Plateau in June 2005 Bisson *et al.* (2007: 182) visited more than 25 caves in the vicinity of Mukhayyat. However, "[...] *our inspections of caves and rock-shelters proved fruitless [...] none of them showing any evidence of artifacts earlier than the Bronze Age. The many caves on the slopes of Mount Nebo have been dug out by shepherds, pilgrims, and treasure hunters looking for the Ark of the Covenant!*" Not quite so: the caves below Mukhayyat were excavated and subsequently published in two volumes by J.A. Ripamonti (1963) and S.J. Saller (1966).

ter encampments in the Jordanian Rift Valley and the higher and cooler areas on the Jordanian Central Plateau or even at the Syrian Steppe.

CONCENTRATIONS OF FINDS

MN 41
UTM coordinates: 759312 East / 3519996 North = 35° 44'18.720" East / 31° 47'9.886" North. Altitude above sea level: 550 metres.

A concentration of flints (c. 20 x 30 metres) from a recently ploughed field east of Wadi 'Uyun Musa. Middle Palaeolithic flints, covered by a yellowish-white patina were dominating, but 15 Upper– Epipalaeolithic flints were also found, all of a grey or reddish brown flint (see below p. 95). 53 Middle Palaeolithic flints were recovered from the site:

3 *Mousterian points* (*Fig. 42 a*)
4 *Levallois points*
1 *fragmentary point* (*Fig. 42 b*)
2 *side-scrapers* (*Fig. 42 c-d*)
1 *end-scraper* made on a fragmentary flake core (*Fig. 42 g*)
2 *small cordiform handaxes*, both with a broken tip and secondarily flaked at the distal end, both with regular edges and a symmetrical longitudinal section. Length 7.3 cm (*Fig. 42 h*) and 9.4 cm
11 *Levallois cores* (*Fig. 42 e*)
9 *Levallois flakes* (*Fig. 42 f*)
5 *fragmentary cores*
15 *flakes*, three of which with irregular retouch/chipping along the edges

MN 93
UTM coordinates: 759083 East / 3519352 North = 35° 44' 9.406" East / 31° 46'49.181" North. Altitude above sea level: 553 metres.

Concentration of flints (c. 15 x 20 metres) from a ploughed field below a conspicuous collapsed shelter facing the north-eastern side of Wadi 'Uyun Musa (*Fig. 43*).
A collection of 51 artefacts of light brown and red-

brown flint, in many cases covered by a yellowish-white patina were recovered from the site:

5 *points* made on flakes (*Fig. 44 f*)
2 *borers* made on flakes
3 *end-scrapers*, one of them made on a Levallois flake (*Fig. 44 c*)
1 *scraper* made on a discoid core (*Fig. 44 d*)
2 *burins* made on flakes
3 *notched flakes*
1 *small Micoquian-style handaxe* with a broken tip. Regular edge and a symmetrical longitudinal section. Length as preserved 7.8 cm (*Fig. 44 g*)
3 *Levallois cores*
2 *Levallois flakes*
1 *bipolar flake core* (*Fig. 44 a*)[20]
1 *discoid flake core* (*Fig. 44 e*)
2 *core fragments*, one of them a "plunging flake" (*Fig. 44 b*)
25 *flakes*, nine of which with irregular retouch/chipping along the edges

MN 209
UTM coordinates: 758700 East / 3514600 North = 35° 43'50.329" East / 31° 44'15.504" North Altitude above sea level 620-640 metres.

A concentration of flints covering a fairly large area in the hills south of 'Ayn Jadidah.
The collection comprises 40 artefacts more than 50% of which are flakes and flake tools struck from Levallois cores. With the exception of 3 pieces of brown flint, the remainder are covered by a white porcelain-like patina:

3 *Mousterian points* (*Fig. 45 a*)
4 *Levallois points* (*Fig. 45 b-d*)
6 *points* with irregular retouch
1 *thick pointed flake*
2 *side-scrapers* (*Fig. 45 g*)
4 *end-scrapers* made on Levallois flakes
2 *small cordiform handaxes*, both with regular edges and a symmetrical longitudinal section. Length 7.8 cm and 9.5 cm (*Fig. 45 h*)
4 *Levallois cores* (*Fig. 45 f*)
4 *Levallois flakes* (*Fig. 45 e*)
4 *irregular flake cores*
6 *irregularly retouched flakes*

[20] The bipolar flake core (*Fig. 44 a*) and the "plunging flake" (*Fig. 44 b*), both made of a reddish-brown flint, might as well represent a later PPNB intrusion.

MN 360

UTM coordinates: 758255 East / 3516045 North = 35° 43'34.810" East / 31° 5'2.570" North. Altitude above sea level: 537 metres.

Concentration of flints from a plateau above the northern side of Wadi Jadidah. Within an area of approximately 30 x 40 metres the artefacts were probably still *in situ* together with chunks of tabular flint (*Figs. 8* and *46-47*).
61 artefacts were collected from the site. With the exception of one pinkish piece (*Fig. 50 b*). They are all made of light brownish – white flint:

3 *Mousterian points* (*Fig. 48 a-b*)
5 *Levallois points* (*Fig. 48 c*)
2 *borers* made on flakes (*Fig. 48 d-e*)
1 *large side-scraper* made on a flake
2 *end-scrapers* made on fragmentary Levallois cores (*Fig. 48 f-g*)
2 *scrapers* with a concavo-convex edge (*Fig. 48 h-i*)
2 *large chopping tools* with cortex partially preserved (*Fig. 50 b-c*), one of them in the shape of a handaxe (*Fig. 50 b*)
4 *Levallois cores*
16 *Levallois flakes* (*Fig. 49 a-e*)
7 *large lumps of roughly worked tabular flint*
4 *irregular flake cores* (*Fig. 50 a*)
4 *core fragments*
9 *flakes*, some of them with irregular retouch/chipping along the edges

MN 466

UTM coordinates: 757543 East / 3519713 North = 35° 43'11.261" East / 31° 47'2.151" North. Altitude above sea level: 385 metres.

A large concentration of flints found within an area of c. 50 x 60 metres at a plateau overlooking the north-western part of Wadi 'Uyun Musa (*Fig. 51*). A collection of 146 light brownish pieces of flint, in most cases covered by a white patina, were recovered from the site:

2 *Mousterian points* (*Fig. 52 a*)
3 *Levallois points* (*Fig. 52 b*)
5 *points made on flakes* (*Fig. 52 c*)
1 *small "pseudo-handaxe"* made on a flake (*Fig. 52 d*)
1 *fragmentary bifacial point* (*Fig. 52 e*)
8 *scrapers* made on flakes (*Fig. 52 g*)
1 *burin* made on a blade (*Fig. 52 f*)

2 *notched flakes*
2 *small, fragmentary handaxes*, one of them with cortex preserved at the rounded proximal butt. *Fig. 54 b*)
2 *discos-shaped bifaces* (*Fig. 54 a*)
1 *small pick* with a triangular section and with cortex preserved at the proximal butt. Length 8.7 cm
6 *chopping tools* (*Fig. 55 a-d*), two of which are secondarily made from broken handaxes (*Fig. 55 c-d*)
2 *fragmentary Levallois cores*
4 *Levallois flakes*
31 *flake cores*, half of which with one striking platform (*Fig. 53 f-i*)
7 *core fragments* (*Fig. 53 d-e*)
68 *flakes*, many of which are irregularly retouched or have use-retouch along the edges (*Fig. 53 a-c*)

MN 520

UTM coordinates: 759660 East / 3519142 North = 35° 44'31.119" East / 31° 46'41.895" North. Altitude above sea level: 525 metres.

A concentration of flints found within an area of c. 40 x 50 metres north-west of 'Uyun Musa, frequently affected by wind erosion (*Figs. 7 and 56*). A collection of 68 pieces of light-brown flint with a white patina and a large amount of crude flint nodules broken into two or three pieces, in some cases with marks from flaking or retouch along the edges was recovered from the site:

4 *Levallois points*
6 *points* made on flakes
1 *side-scraper*
3 *end-scrapers* made on flakes
2 *notched flakes*
1 *small "pseudo-handaxe"* made on a flake. Length 7.1 cm
2 *discos-shaped bifaces*
7 *Levallois flakes*
7 *flake cores*
3 *core fragments*
32 *flakes*, some of which were retouched/chipped along the edges

MN 528

UTM coordinates: 758435 East / 3520200 North = 35° 43'45.604" East / 31° 47'17.223" North. Altitude above sea level: 380 metres.

Concentration of flints from a terrace of gravel and stones north-east of Wadi 'Uyun Musa, gently sloping towards south. The flints were found within an area of approximately 40 x 60 metres (*Fig. 57*). A collection of 73 light greyish-brown to white pieces of flint more than half of which were based on a prepared platform:

1 Mousterian point
15 Levallois points (*Fig. 58 a-b*)
5 points made on flakes (*Fig. 58 c-d*)
1 borer made on a Levallois flake (*Fig. 58 e*)
2 borers made on flakes (*Fig. 58 f-g*)
3 side-scrapers, two of which are made on Levallois flakes (*Fig. 58 h-i*)
4 end-scrapers made on flakes
1 small bifacial "pseudo-handaxe" (*Fig. 58 l*)
5 Levallois cores (*Fig. 58 m-n*)
19 Levallois flakes, half of which are irregularly retouched
4 flake cores
13 flakes and blades (*Fig. 58 j-k*)

MN 581
UTM coordinates 757569 East / 3516116 North = 35° 43'8.832" East / 31° 45'5.433" North.
Altitude above sea level: 500 metres.

A concentration of flints found within an area of c. 50 x 50 metres on a hill north of Wadi Jadidah, sloping down towards south. The collection comprises 40 Middle Palaeolithic artefacts covered by a yellowish-white patina and 29 Upper– Epipalaeolithic grey-greyish-brown flints (see below p. 96). A collection of 40 artefacts, all of a light greyish-brown flint with a yellowish white patina, was recovered from the site:

1 Levallois point
1 end-scraper made on a flake
1 notched flake
10 Levallois cores
5 Levallois flakes
4 large flint nodules with partly preserved cortex and with irregular scars from flakes having been struck off the nodules
2 flake cores
16 flakes, some of them with irregular retouch

MN 733
UTM coordinates: 759025 East / 3517056 North = 35° 44'5.010"East / 31° 45'34.741" North.
Altitude above sea level: 753 metres.

A concentration of flints found on a sloping hillside north of Wadi Jadidah within an area of 10 x 20 metres. A collection of 49 artefacts made of light greyish-brown flint, all badly worn from erosion, was recovered from the site:

2 Levallois points
2 small points made on flakes
8 side-scrapers made on large flakes
2 end-scrapers made on cores
1 notched flake
2 small cordiform handaxes. Length 8.0 cm and 9.8 cm
1 fragment of a handaxe, lower part
4 Levallois cores
4 Levallois flakes
4 flake cores
19 flakes, some of them irregularly retouched/chipped

SCATTERS OF FINDS

MN 15
UTM coordinates: 758312 East / 3521110 North = 35° 43'41.800" East / 31° 47' 46.846" North.
Altitude above sea level: 499 metres.

11 pieces of flint picked up from a ploughed field above the northern side of Wadi 'Uyun Musa:

2 thick points
2 Levallois cores
1 fragmentary Levallois core
2 Levallois flakes
1 flake core
3 flakes

MN 16
UTM coordinates: 758618 East / 3521307 North = 35° 43'53.612" East / 31° 47.52.987" North.
Altitude above sea level: 522 metres.

5 pieces of flint picked up from a ploughed field on a hill sloping down towards the northern side of Wadi 'Uyun Musa:

1 Levallois point
1 end-scraper with a steep retouch
1 globular nodule
1 flake core
1 retouched flake

MN 31

UTM coordinates: 760200 East / 3519970 North = 35° 44'52.422" East / 31° 47'8.4948" North. Altitude above sea level: 610 metres.

11 pieces of flint picked up from an exposed rocky surface between two megalithic tombs (**MN 30** and **MN 32**) north-east of 'Uyun Musa:

1 *Levallois point*
2 *small discoid bifaces*, diameter 3.9 and 6.1 cm
2 *Levallois cores*
2 *Levallois flakes*
4 *retouched flakes*

MN 34

UTM coordinates: 759383 East / 3519142 North = 35°44'20.599" East / 31°46'42.123" North. Altitude above sea level: 537 metres.

A small collection of 26 flints from a hilltop north-west of 'Uyun Musa:

1 *Levallois core*
10 *flake cores*
2 *core fragments*
1 *primary core tablet*
2 *secondary core tablets*
10 *flakes*, half of them with irregular retouch/chipping

MN 45

UTM coordinates 759175 East / 3520178 North = 35° 44'13.690" East / 31° 47'15.903" North. Altitude above sea level: 420 metres.

7 pieces of flint picked up from a hill sloping down towards Wadi 'Uyun Musa:

2 *Mousterian points*
2 *slightly retouched points*
1 *globular chopping tool*
2 *retouched flakes*

MN 72

UTM coordinates 758460 East / 3520100 North = 35° 43'46.459" East / 35° 47'14.136" North. Altitude above sea level: 380 metres.

28 flints picked up within a large area at a plateau between megalithic tombs **MN 67-72**. The collection comprises 22 Middle Palaeolithic flints, all with a yel-lowish white patina, and 10 Upper– Epipalaeolithic flints of a light greyish colour (see below p. 95):

4 *Levallois points*
1 *side-scraper*
2 *end-scrapers*
3 *Levallois cores*
3 *primary core tablets*
1 *secondary core tablet*
3 *retouched flakes*

MN 356

UTM coordinates: 758348 East / 3515668 North = 35° 43'37.983" East / 31° 44'50.264" North. Altitude above sea level: 487 metres.

29 pieces of flint picked up from a ploughed field on the northern brink of Wadi Jadidah:

4 *borers*
3 *side-scrapers*
2 *notched flakes*
5 *Levallois flakes*
1 *bifacial flake core*
6 *flake cores*
2 *retouched flakes*
6 *retouched blades*

MN 363

UTM coordinates: 758430 East / 3516234 North = 35° 43'41.635" East / 31° 45'8.559" North. Altitude above sea level: 635 metres.

25 pieces of flint picked up from a large area (c. 200 x 200 metres) from a plateau north of Wadi Jadidah:

1 *end-of-blade scraper*
7 *Levallois flakes*
7 *flake cores*
10 *flakes with irregular retouch*

MN 383

UTM coordinates: 758141 East / 3515635 North = 35° 43'30.092" East / 31° 44'49.362" North. Altitude above sea level: 458 metres.

23 pieces of flint collected from a narrow plateau, now overhanging the northern brink of Wadi Jadidah. The plateau was presumably formed by soil washed down and secondarily deposited from a higher ter-race along the river:

1 Mousterian point
1 point
1 side-scraper made on a Levallois flake
1 end-scraper
1 Levallois core
1 Levallois flake
3 flake cores
4 core fragments
10 flakes, half of which were irregularly retouched

MN 385

UTM coordinates: 757862 East / 3515961 North
= 35° 43'19.809" East / 31° 45'0.166" North.
Altitude above sea level: 512 metres.

28 pieces of flint from a plateau on the northern
brink of Wadi Jadidah:

1 Levallois point
1 side-scraper
1 chopping tool, with a rounded but
2 Levallois cores
5 Levallois flakes
4 flake cores
1 blade core
13 flakes, some of them with irregular retouch

MN 409

UTM coordinates: 756890 East / 3516370 North
= 35° 42'43.294" East / 31° 45'14.3964" North.
Altitude above sea level: 310 metres.

18 pieces of flint picked up from a rocky terrace sloping down towards the northern side of 'Ayn Kanisah:

2 Mousterian points
1 side-scraper
2 Levallois flakes
4 large flake cores
9 flakes

MN 432

UTM coordinates: 754255 East / 3516345 North
= 35° 41'3.217" East / 31° 45'15.7068" North.
Altitude above sea level: 230 metres.

A collection of 13 heavily worn and patinated flints
from a terrace near the southwestern edge of
Wadi Kanisah – only a hundred metres from the
single-found handaxe **MN 433** (*Fig. 40 c,* see
above p. 47).

2 Mousterian points
2 Levallois points
1 point
2 end-scrapers
3 chopping tools
3 retouched flakes

MN 456

UTM coordinates: 755203 East / 3520169 North
= 35° 41'42.812" East / 31° 47'18.843" North.
Altitude above sea level: 128 metres.

14 flints picked up from a surface of gravel and
larger stones on a terrace along the south-western
edge of Wadi 'Uyun Musa:

1 Levallois point
3 Levallois cores
10 Levallois flakes

MN 483

UTM coordinates: 757773 East / 3519408 North
= 35° 43'19.706" East / 31° 46'52.069" North.
Altitude above sea level: 397 metres.

28 flints, all covered by a white patina, picked up
from a terrace sloping down towards the north-
eastern edge of Wadi 'Uyun Musa:

2 Levallois points
3 points
2 notched flakes
3 small bifacially retouched points
1 small irregular handaxe. Length 10 cm
3 Levallois cores
5 Levallois flakes
7 flakes cores
2 flakes

MN 486

UTM coordinates: 757734 East / 3519608 North
= 35° 43'18.415" East / 31° 46'58.589" North.
Altitude above sea level: 366 metres.

8 pieces of flint from a terrace north-east of Wadi
'Uyun Musa:

1 notched flake
2 Levallois flakes
3 core fragments
2 flakes

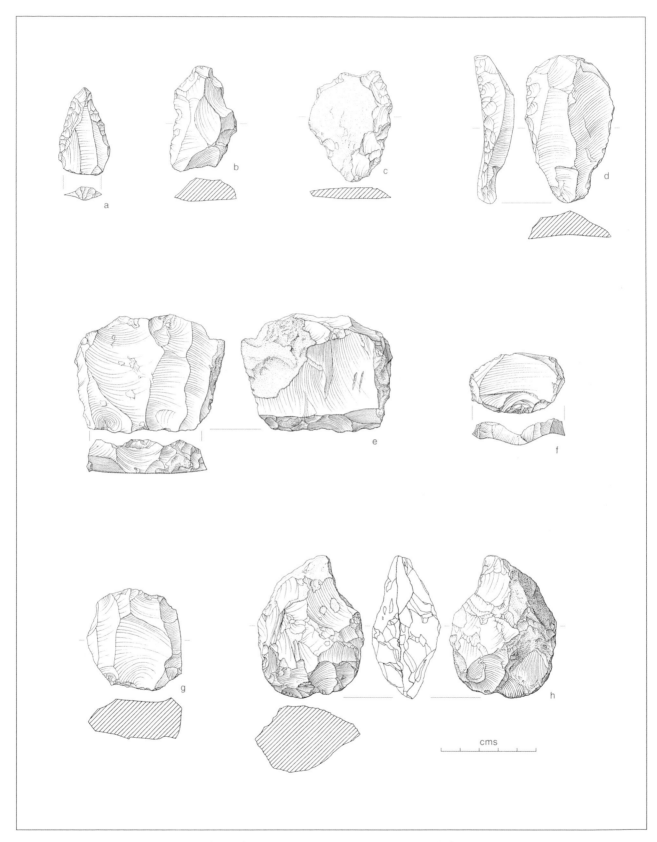

❱ Fɪɢ. 42 Middle Palaeolithic artefacts from **MN 41**: Mousterian point (**a**), fragmentary point (**b**), side scrapers (**c-d**), fragmentary Levallois core (**e**), Levallois flake (**f**), end-scarper made on a fragmentary flake core (**g**), handaxe (**h**).

❱ Fɪɢ. 43 View towards north across the Middle Palaeolithic site **MN 93** in front of the wall of rock, still with visible remains of a collapsed shelter. September 2008.

❯ Fig. 46 View towards south-east across the Middle Palaeolithic site **MN 360**. The artefacts are still *in situ* together with chunks of flint. September 1994.

❯ FIG. 47 Chunk of tabular flint from the Middle Palaeolithic site **MN 360** *in situ*. September 1994.

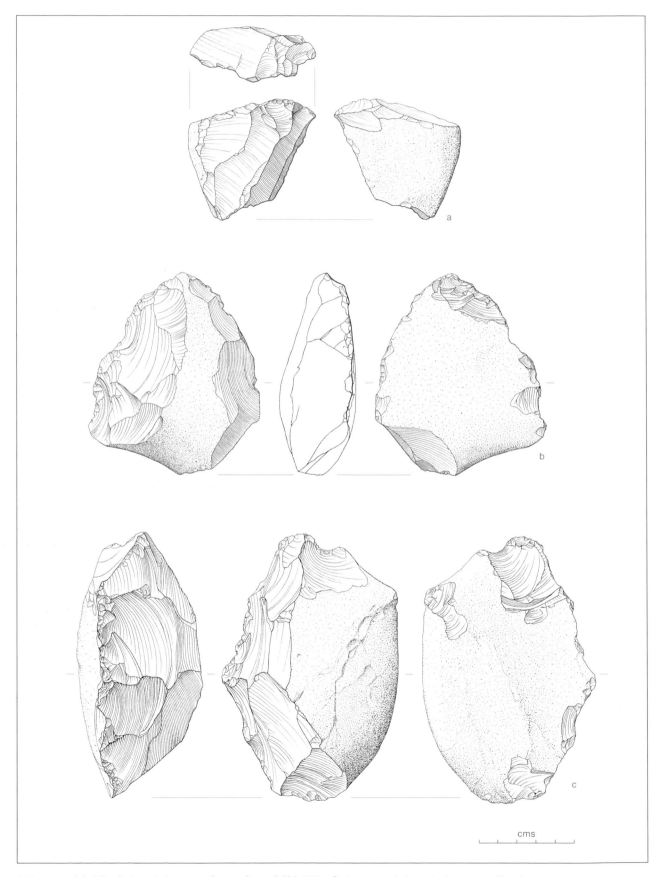

cms

) Fig. 50 Middle Palaeolithic artefacts from **MN 360**: flake core (**a**) and choppers (**b-c**).

❯ Fɪɢ. 51 View towards north across the Middle Palaeolithic site **MN 466**. September 1995.

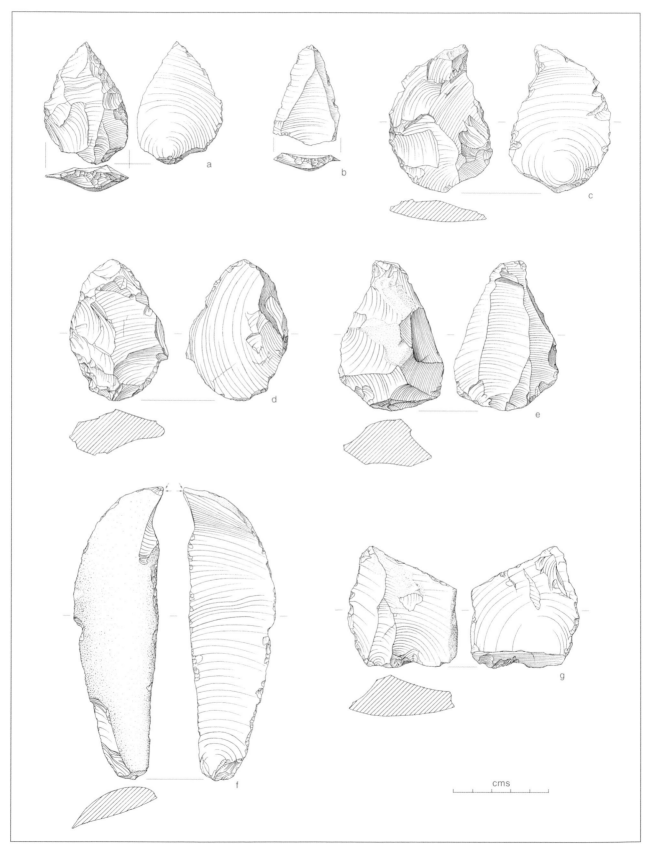

❱ Fɪɢ. 52 Middle Palaeolithic artefacts from **MN 466**: Mousterian point (**a**), Levallois point (**b**), points made on a flakes (**c-d**), fragmentary bifacial point (**e**), burin made on a blade (**f**), and a side scraper made on a flake (**g**).

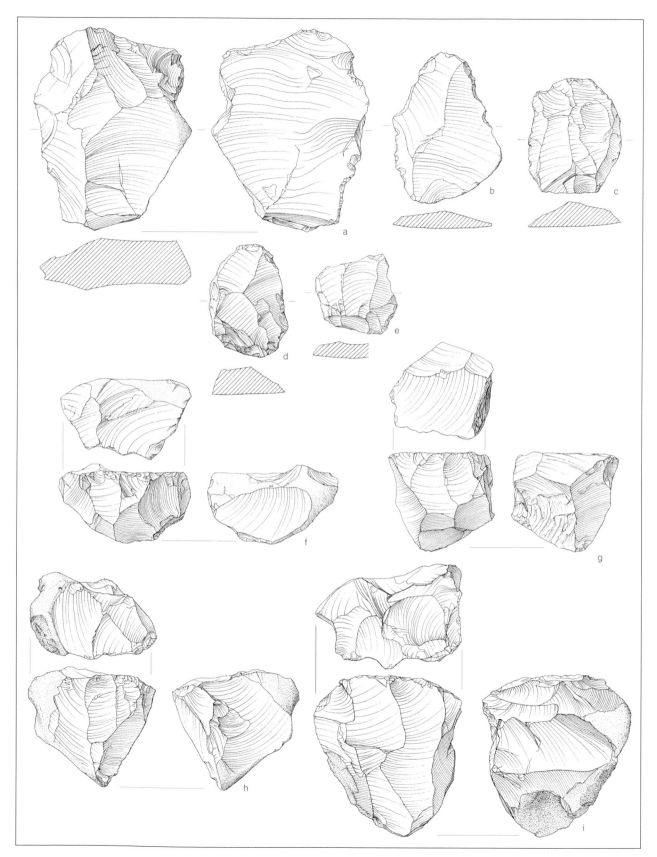

❱ FIG. 53 Middle Palaeolithic artefacts from **MN 466**: retouched flakes (**a-d**), core fragment (**e**), and flake cores (**f-i**).

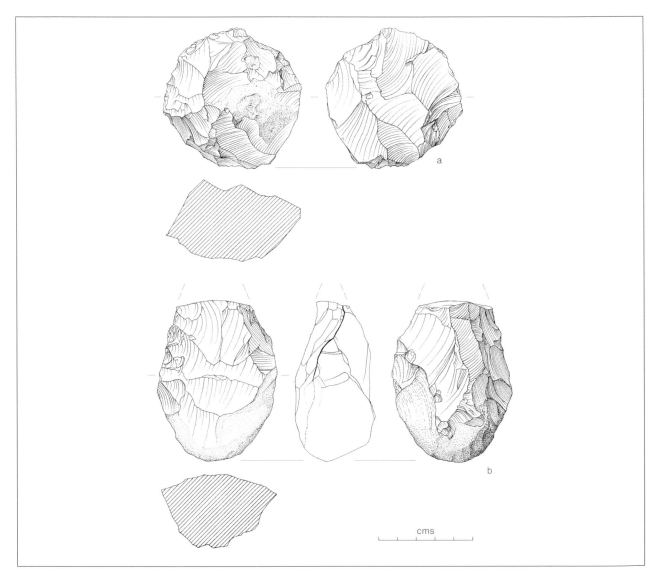

❯ FIG. 54 Middle Palaeolithic artefacts from **MN 466**: discos-shaped biface (**a**) and a handaxe (**b**).

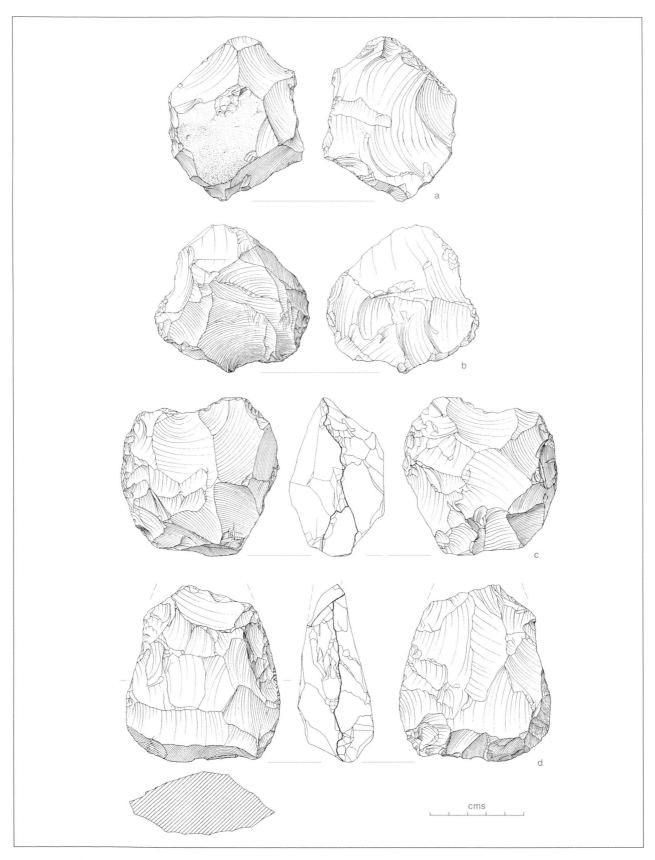

❱ FIG. 55 Middle Palaeolithic artefacts from **MN 466**: chopping tools (**a-d**), two of which are made from broken handaxes (**c-d**).

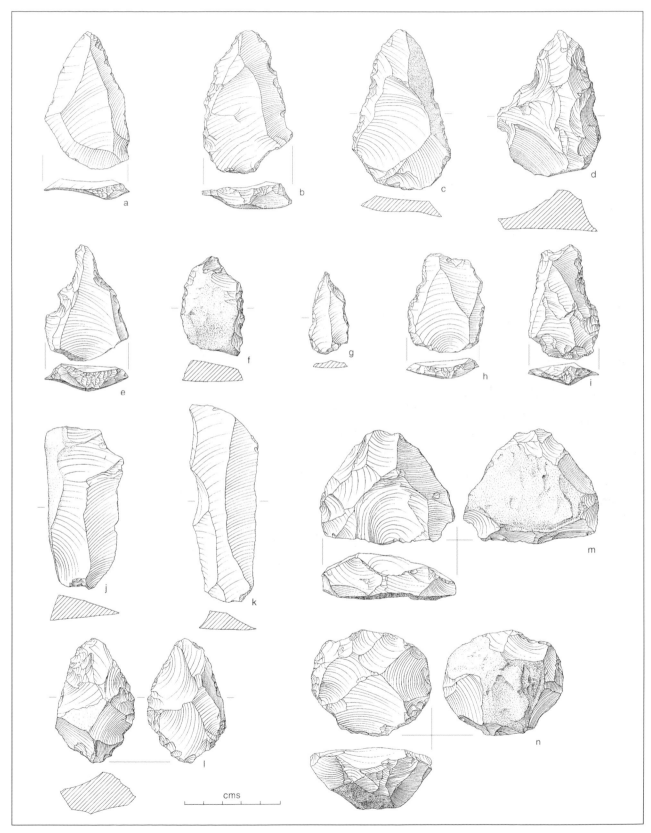

❱ Fɪɢ. 58 Middle Palaeolithic artefacts from **MN 528**: Levallois points, slightly modified by retouch (**a-b**), points made on flakes (**c-d**), borers (**e-g**), side scrapers made on a prepared platform (**h-i**), flakes (**j-k**), bifacial scraper (**l**), small triangular Levallois core (**m**), and a discoid flake core with a prepared platform (**n**).

❭ Fɪɢ. 59 View towards east across the Middle Palaeolithic site **MN 647**. September 1997.

MN 378

UTM coordinates: 758103 East / 3516045 North
= 35° 43'29.039" East / 31° 45'2.694" North.
Altitude above sea level: 550 metres.

26 pieces of reddish-brown flint picked up from a
hillside north of 'Ayn Jadidah, below a collapsed
shelter facing SE:

3 small end-scrapers
2 side-scrapers
2 borers
1 small notched flake
1 notched blade
1 notched microblade
1 denticulated blade
3 small core fragments
1 core tablet
6 irregularly retouched flakes
5 irregularly retouched blades

MN 499

UTM coordinates: 758886 East / 3518125 North
= 35° 44'0.753" East / 31° 46'9.536" North.
Altitude above sea level: 605 metres.

28 greyish-brown pieces of flint picked up from a
hillside south of 'Uyun Musa:

3 scrapers
1 borer
3 micropoints/awls
6 small flake cores
2 microblade cores
4 microblades
4 microflakes
2 irregularly retouched flakes
3 blades

MN 576

UTM coordinates: 757224 East / 3516163 North
= 35° 42'55.777" East / 31° 45'7.238" North.
Altitude above sea level: 430 metres.

30 flints picked up from a terrace north of Wadi Jadidah within an area of approximately 20 x 20 metres around the collapsed remains of a megalithic
tomb (**MN 576**):

3 small borers
5 small flake cores

4 retouched flakes
3 flakes
1 blade
4 microblades
10 chips

MN 578

UTM coordinates: 757363 East / 3516218 North
= 35° 43'1.107" East / 31° 45'8.909" North.
Altitude above sea level: 473 metres.

31 dark greyish-brown flints picked up from a terrace north of Wadi Jadidah:

6 end-scrapers made on flakes
8 borers made on small flakes
1 notched blade
2 large, backed blades/knives
5 large flake cores
2 small flake cores
1 core fragment
3 microblade cores
1 microblade
2 chips

MN 581

UTM coordinates: 757569 East / 3516116 North
= 35° 43'8.832" East / 31° 45'5.433" North.
Altitude above sea level: 500 metres.

29 pieces of greyish-brown flint picked up at a hill
north of Wadi Jadidah, sloping down towards
south. 40 Middle Palaeolithic artefacts were also
collected at the location (see above p. 67):

4 scrapers with a concavo-convex edge
7 end-scrapers
5 borers
2 notched blades
4 microblades
4 small flake cores
3 retouched flakes

MN 589

UTM coordinates: 756997 East / 3516356 North
= 35° 42'47.341" East / 31° 45'13.684" North.
Altitude above sea level: 370 metres.

7 pieces of flint picked up from a hillside sloping
down towards the north-western side of Wadi

Jadidah. The collection also comprises 8 Middle Palaeolithic flints (see above p. 70):

1 scraper with a concavo-convex edge
1 microblade
3 small core fragments
2 chips

MN 630
UTM coordinates: 756027 East / 3517218 North = 35° 42'11.324" East / 31° 45'42.4362" North. Altitude above sea level: 511 metres.

19 pieces of greyish-brown flint, picked up together with 2 Middle Palaeolithic flints from a plateau near the edge of a terrace overlooking the Jordan Valley and the Dead Sea (see above p. 71):

4 end-scrapers made on flakes
2 notched flakes
3 notched blades
2 small flake cores
3 fragmentary blade cores
5 chips

MN 645
UTM coordinates: 756892 East / 3517218 North = 35° 42'44.960" East / 31° 46'8.760" North. Altitude above sea level: 506 metres.

28 pieces of flint collected from a terrace on the slopes west of Siyagha:

1 thumbnail scraper
1 end-scraper made on a microblade
3 notched flakes
5 small flake cores
1 primary core platform
14 flakes with irregular retouch
3 chips

MN 649
UTM coordinates: 757209 East / 3518233 North = 35° 42'57.170" East / 31° 46'14.407" North. Altitude above sea level: 487 metres.

9 greyish brown flints picked up from a terrace west of Siyagha:

1 borer made on a flake
2 notched blades

1 micropoint/awl
2 small flake cores
1 fragmentary core
1 retouched flake
1 irregularly retouched blade

MN 665
UTM coordinates: 765814 East / 3517594 North = 35° 42'3.591" East / 31° 45'54.807" North. Altitude above sea level: 601 metres.

16 pieces of greyish-brown flint picked up from a hilltop west of Siyagha:

1 end-scraper made on a flake
3 small borers made on flakes
1 backed blade/knife
1 small flake core
4 core fragments
6 flakes with irregular retouch

MN 673
UTM coordinates: 757528 East / 3517728 North = 35° 43'8.805" East / 31° 45'57.764" North. Altitude above sea level: 670 metres.

9 pieces of grey flint from a hillside south-west of Siyagha (*Fig. 86*). The collection also comprises 13 Middle Palaeolithic and 70 PPNB flints (see pp. 70 and 119):

1 thumbnail scraper
2 small flake cores
4 fragmentary cores
2 microblade cores

MN 748
UTM coordinates: 759665 East / 3515347 North = 35° 44'27.679" East / 31° 44'38.837" North. Altitude above sea level: 710 metres.

13 pieces of grey flint collected from a terrace at the southern edge of Mukhayyat, north of 'Ayn Jadidah:

2 small borers
2 microborers/awls
2 small flake cores
6 slightly retouched flakes
1 retouched blade

❭ FIG. 61 View towards west with the Epipalaeolithic site **MN 18** in front of the hill in the middle of the picture. On top of the hill are the remains of a circular megalithic tomb (**MN 17**). September 1993.

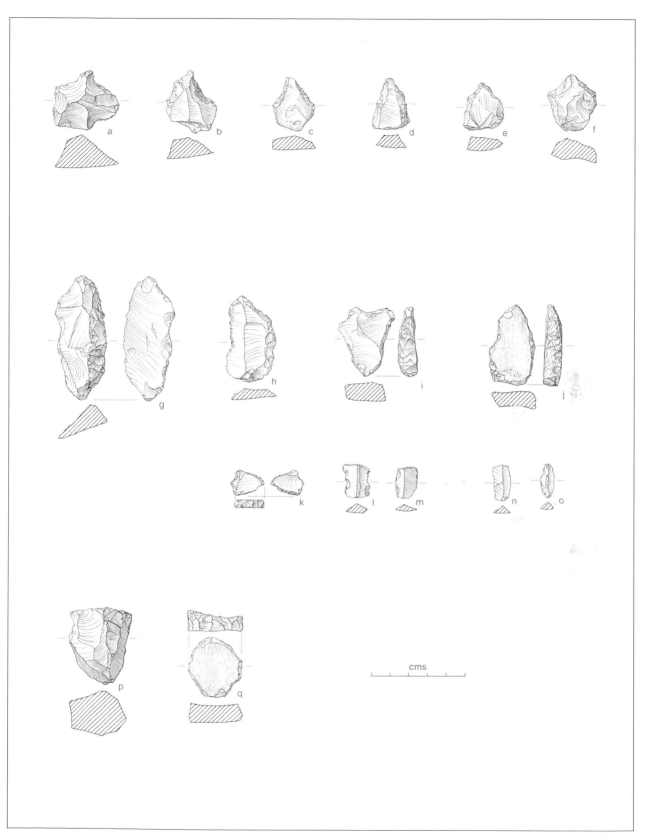

) FIG. 62 Epipalaeolithic artefacts from **MN 18**: borers (**a-d**) and borers/nosed scrapers (**e-f**), notched flake (**g**), side scrapers (**h** and **j**), scraper with a concavo-convex edge (**i**), triangular microscraper (**k**), microblades (**l-o**), flake core (**p**), and a core-tablet (**q**).

❭ FIG. 63 View towards south across the Epipalaeolithic site **MN 29** with the remains of a megalithic tomb in the background (**MN 30**). September 1993.

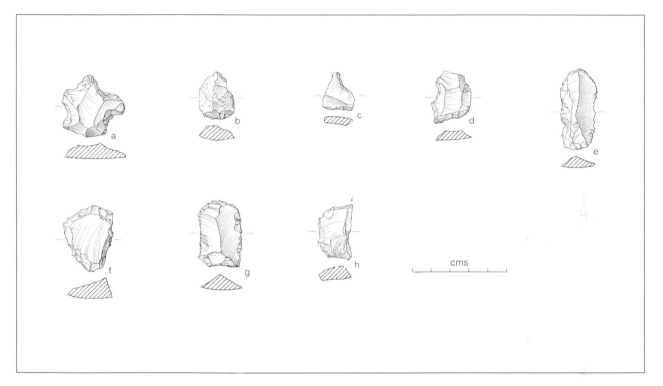

❯ FIG. 64 Epipalaeolithic artefacts from **MN 29**: scraper with a concavo-convex edge (**a**), borers (**b-d**), notched blade (**e**), end scrapers (**f-g**), and a burin (**h**).

❯ FIG. 67 View towards east with the Epipalaeolithic site **MN 455** on top of the plateau in the middle of the picture. September 1995.

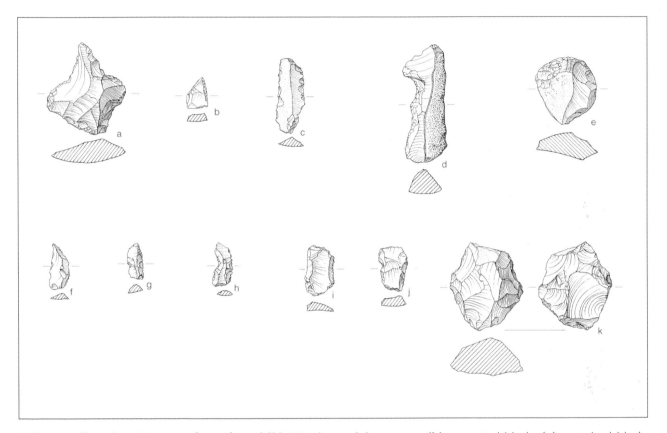

▶ Fɪɢ. 68 Epipalaeolithic artefacts from **MN 455**: borer (**a**), trapeze (**b**), serrated blade (**c**), notched blade (**d**), end scraper (**e**), microborer (**f**), retouched microblades (**g-h**), retouched, trapeze-like flakes (**i-j**), and a flake core (**k**).

❯ FIG. 71 View towards south-west across Epipalaeolithic site **MN 574**. September 1997.

❭ FIG. 72 View towards south of Epipalaeolithic site **MN 588** in front of a collapsed shelter. September 1997.

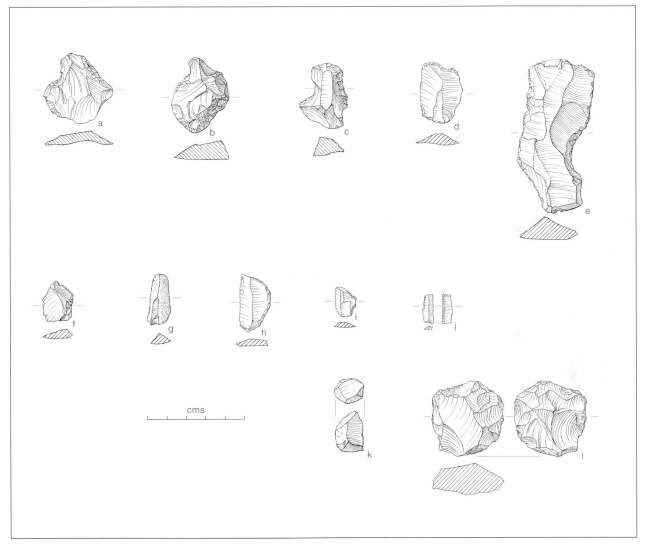

❯ Fɪɢ. 73 Epipalaeolithic artefacts from **MN 588**: borers (**a-b**), scrapers (**c-d**), notched flake (**e**), retouched flake (**f**), blade (**g**), lunate (**h**), micro-burin (**i**), backed bladelet (**j**), core tablet (**k**), and a discoid, bifacial flake core (**l**).

❯ Fɪɢ. 74 View of Epipalaeolithic site **MN 646** in front of a shelter facing north-west. September 1997.

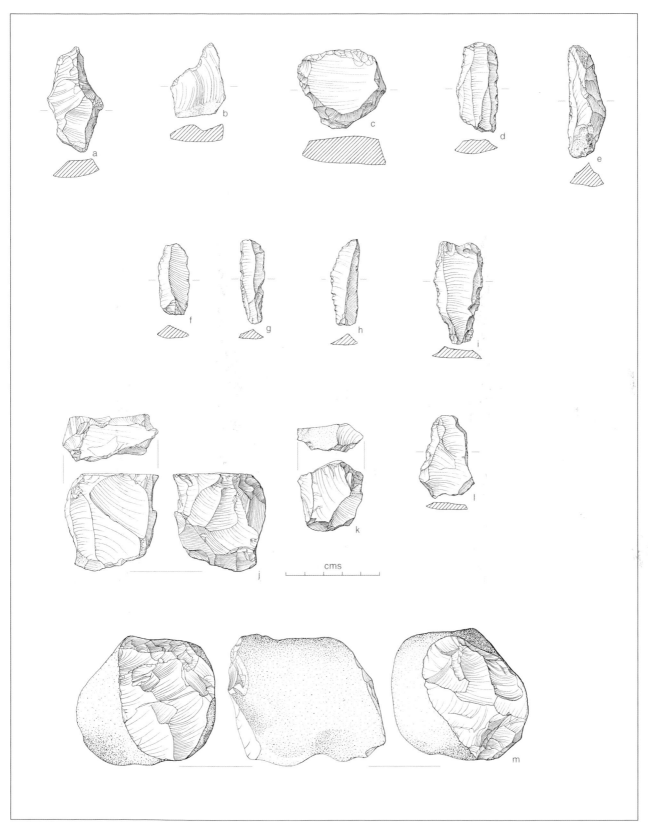

❱ Fɪɢ. 75 Epipalaeolithic artefacts from **MN 646**: borers (**a-b**), scrapers (**c-d**), secondary crest blade (**e**), re-touched blade (**f**), backed blades (**g-h**) truncated blade with a tang (**i**), flake cores (**j-k**), notched flake (**l**), and a partly flaked chunk of flint (**m**).

❯ FIG. 76 View of the Epipalaeolithic site **MN 672**, located on the hillside and the plateau in front of it, facing south. September 1997.

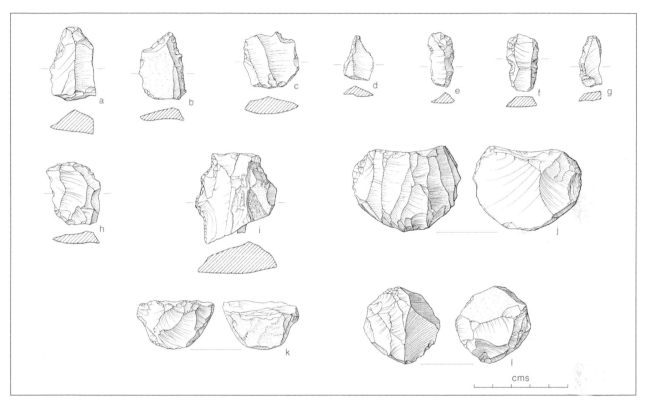

❭ FIG. 77 Epipalaeolithic artefacts from **MN 672**: borers (**a-d**), notched blades (**e-f**), blade with irregular re-touch (**g**), scraper (**h**), notched flake (**i**), and blade-and flake cores (**j-l**).

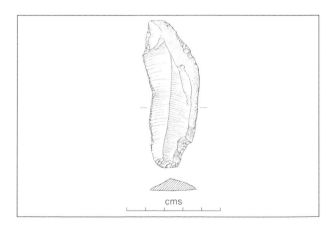

❭ FIG. 78 Single-shouldered knife from the Upper Palaeolithic site **MN 328**.

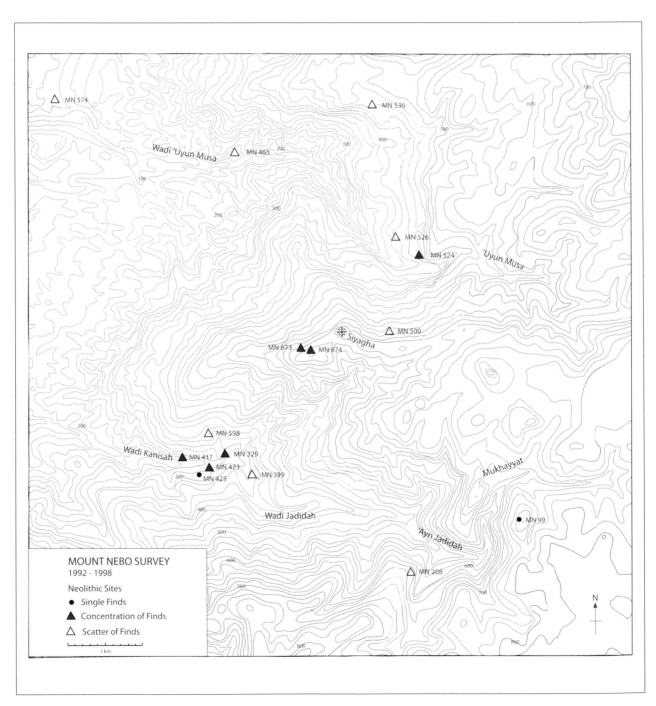

MOUNT NEBO SURVEY
1992 - 1998

Neolithic Sites
● Single Finds
▲ Concentration of Finds
△ Scatter of Finds

1 km

❭ FIG. 79 Map showing the distribution of Neolithic sites.

) THE NEOLITHIC PERIODS (

During the Mount Nebo survey 13 Pre-Pottery Neolithic sites and single finds were located (*Fig. 79*). Typical of the PPNB inventory from these sites are: naviform flake- and blade cores (*Figs. 82 e-g, 85 a-c and 87 a-c*), primary and secondary crestblades and core tablets (*Figs. 82 h-k, 85 f-j, and 90*), tanged arrowheads (*Figs. 81 a-d and 84 a-c*), and blades with sickle-gloss (*Figs. 81 g-i and 84 k-l*). The inventory also includes borers, scrapers, burins, notched blades, picks, a large polished axe, pestles and a fragmentary bowl of basalt. As previously mentioned most of the Pre-Pottery Neolithic artefacts were made from a pinkish-red or brown flint (cf. p. 63).

Two of the PPNB sites were low tells, both located near water, above the right bank of Wadi Kanisah (**MN 417**, *Fig. 80*) and the right bank of Wadi 'Uyun Musa (**MN 524**, *Fig. 83*). The inventory is fairly rich and varied (*Figs. 81-82 and 84-85*). The shape of the arrowheads (*Fig. 84 a-d*) and the two picks (*Fig. 84 f-g*) from **MN 524** might possibly suggest a slightly later date for this settlement than **MN 417**.

Two concentrations of flint located within a distance of c. 150 metres from each other on the hills south-west of Siyagha (**MN 673**, *Fig. 86* and **MN 674**, *Figs. 88-89*) are characterized by a dominance of raw materials and débitage compared to tools (*Fig. 87*). Furthermore, the presence of a natural outcrop of pinkish flint at **MN 674** might support an interpretation of these two sites, which are located in the hills just between the two wadies, as temporary open-air sites used for the extraction of flint and as workshops for the production of tools.

Scatters (**MN 208**, **MN 399**, **MN 465**, **MN 500**, **MN 536**, **MN 574**, and **MN 598**) and single finds (**MN 99** and **MN 425**) of PPNB flints are primarily found on hills and terraces along the two wadi systems (cf. the map *Fig. 79*). In this context it is interesting to note that several of the Neolithic sites are located very close to water on the brinks of Wadi Kanisah, in contrast to a concentration of Upper– Epipalaeolithic occupations by hunter-gatherers, found more easterly in rock-shelters and on terraces in the hills north of Wadi Jadidah (cf. the map *Fig. 60*).

Chronologically, the lithic materials from the Pre-Pottery Neolithic sites located at Mount Nebo suggest a date within the Middle PPNB phase (c. 10,000 – 9,500 years bp).[26]

Two small Pottey Neolithic tells (**MN 329**, *Figs. 91-92* and **MN 423**, *Fig. 95*) were both situated near the wadi bed, facing each other, on either side of Wadi Kanisah. The inventory picked up from the surface of the two tells suggests that they were contemporary and that they may in fact represent one settlement, just divided by the stream of water in Wadi Kanisah.

The lithics included tanged arrowheads (*Figs. 93 d-f* and *96 a-b*), sickle segments (*Figs. 93 p* and *96 e-h*), points made on cores (*Fig. 94 a-b*), flake- and blade cores with one striking platform (*Fig. 94 c-d*), all of a dark greyish-brown flint – in contrast to the pinkish flint used in PPNB contexts.[27] A fragmentary pestle and a large hoe made from basalt was also found (*Fig. 94 i*). The pottery was all of a straw-tempered buff ware, including sherds with

---

[26] Cf. Mortensen 1970; Gebel and Kozlowski 1994: 387 ff.; Rollefson 2008: 75 ff.

[27] It is interesting that a similar change in lithic raw materials was observed by Gary Rollefson at the transition from the PPNC to the Yarmukian at Ayn Ghazal: *"The use of high-quality Wadi Huwayjir-type flint with pink-to-purple hues disappeared altogether, although some of the projectile points and sickle blades appear to have been made on pink-purple flint naviform blades scavenged from earlier cultural deposits at Ayn Ghazal"* (Rollefson 2008: 95).

plastic decoration (*Figs. 93 c* and *96 i*), sherds with a cream coloured decoration on a dark red slip (*Fig. 93 b*) and with a red-painted decoration on a cream slip (*Fig. 96 j*) similar to pottery from the so-called Pottery Neolithic A / Jericho IX-phase. Furthermore, sherds with an incised herring-bone decoration (*Fig. 93 a*) in one case above red-painted bands (*Fig. 96 m*), related to the earlier Yarmukian tradition, also oc-curred.[28] The pottery seems to fall within the late Yarmukian and the early Pottery Neolithic A tradition (c. 7,000 – 6,000 years bp), possibly leaving a gap of more than 1500 years between the Pre-pottery and the Pottery Neolithic occupation of the Nebo region.

A small collection of Pottery Neolithic sherds and flints was found north of 'Uyun Musa at what has probably been a low tell (**MN 526**). The site was badly destroyed by bulldozers and agricultural activities. The finds suggest that the occupation may have been contemporary with the two tells in Wadi Kanisah (**MN 329** and **MN 423**).

CONCENTRATIONS OF PRE-POTTERY NEOLITHIC FINDS

MN 417

UTM coordinates: 756048 East / 3516310 North = 35° 42'11.265" East / 31° 45'12.961" North. Altitude above sea level: 305 metres.

153 pieces of pinkish flint picked up from the sur-face of a low tell in a garden on the northern edge of Wadi Kanisah (*Fig. 80*). The extension of the tell is c. 70 x 70 metres, the height c. 2.5 metres:

2 arrowheads (Fig. 81 a-b)
3 tanged flakes (Fig. 81 c-d)
4 scrapers made on thick flakes with a steep edge (Fig. 81 l-m)
1 borer on a flake (Fig. 81 e)
5 notched blades (Fig. 81 f)
4 notched flakes
5 burins (Fig. 81 j-k), one of them made on a sickle-blade (Fig. 81 i)
2 sickle-blades (Fig. 81 g-h)
3 small flake cores
8 naviform flake- and blade cores (Fig. 82 e-g)

5 fragmentary blade cores
3 primary crest blades (Fig. 82 h-i)
4 secondary crest blades (Fig. 82 j)
2 primary core tablets (Fig. 82 k)
2 secondary core tablets
19 flakes
57 blades and blade segments (Fig. 82 a-d)
24 microblades
In addition: *1 pestle made of basalt*
1 large axe of chipped and polished stone (Fig. 82 l)

MN 524

UTM coordinates: 759095 East / 3519018 North = 35° 44'9.543" East / 31° 46'38.336" North. Altitude above sea level: 460 metres.

225 pieces of light grey to reddish-brown flint from the surface of a low tell in a garden on the northern side of Wadi 'Uyun Musa, 8-10 metres above the wadi bed (*Fig. 83*). The extension of the site is ap-proximately 40 x 90 metres:

4 fragmentary arrowheads (Fig. 84 a-c)
9 end-scrapers made on flakes (Fig. 84 p-q)
13 borers made on blades and small flakes (Fig. 84 d-e)
1 pick with a triangular section made on a thick flake (Fig. 84 j)
1 bifacial pick made on a core (Fig. 84 g)
12 notched blades and flakes (Fig. 84 h-j)
4 burins made on blades (Fig. 84 m-o)
3 sickleblades (Fig. 84 k-l)
1 knife on a truncated blade (Fig. 84 r)
1 tanged blade (Fig. 84 s)
10 naviform blade- and flake cores (Fig. 85 a-c)
9 fragmentary naviforn cores
7 small flake- and blade cores with one platform (Fig. 85 d-e)
5 primary crest blades (Fig. 85 g-j)
2 secondary crest blades
5 primary core tablets (Fig. 85 f)
2 secondary core tablets
53 flakes, some of them with irregular retouch
74 blades, half of them with irregular retouch (Fig. 84 t-u)
9 chips
In addition: *1 fragment of a basalt bowl*
2 fragmentary pestles

---

[28] Cf. Kenyon and Holland 1982; Bossut, Kafafi and Dollfus 1988: 128-130; Rollefson 2008: 95-99.

MN 673

UTM coordinates: 757528 East / 3517728 North = 35° 43'8.805" East / 31° 45'57.764" North. Altitude above sea level: 670 metres.

70 light grey to pinkish pieces of flint picked up from a hillside south-west of Siyagha (*Fig. 86*). The collection also comprises 13 Middle Palae-olithic and 9 pieces of Upper– Epipalaeolithic flint. (see above pp. 71 and 97).

1 end-of-blade scraper
7 small flake- and blade cores with one platform
4 naviform blade cores (Fig. 87 a-c)
9 fragmentary naviform cores
2 primary crest blades
5 primary core tablets
24 flakes, more than half of them modified by retouch
18 blades, some of them with irregular retouch

MN 674

UTM coordinates: 757731 East / 3517644 North = 35° 43'16.434" East / 31° 45'54.874" East. Altitude above sea level: 720 metres.

A concentration of 86 pieces of flint picked up from a hill south-west of Siyagha, c. 150 metres east of MN 673 (*Figs. 88-89*):

3 scrapers made on flakes
3 scrapers made on cores
9 points made on flakes
1 lump of tabular flint
5 small flake- and blade cores with one platform
3 naviform blade cores
1 core fragment
2 primary crest blades
3 secondary crest blades
3 primary core tablets
20 flakes, some of them retouched
24 blades, some with irregular retouch
9 chips

PRE-POTTERY NEOLITHIC SCATTERS OF FINDS AND SINGLE FINDS

MN 99

UTM coordinates: 760470 East / 3515570 North = 35° 44'58.452" East / 31° 44'45.528" North. Altitude above sea level: c. 815 metres.

1 sickleblade made on a primary crest blade (Fig. 90) picked up by Michele Piccirillo north of the Iron Age II tower at Khirbat al-Mukhayyat.

MN 208

UTM coordinates: 758894 East / 3514555 North = 35° 43'57.651" East / 31° 44'13.709" North. Altitude above sea level: 695 metres.

14 pieces of flint picked up from an area covering c. 10 x 20 metres on a hill south of 'Ayn Jadidah:

1 end-scraper made on a flake
2 typical PPNB borers made on blades
3 notched blades
1 small flake core
1 fragmentary naviform core
1 secondary crest blade
2 blades made on bipolar cores
2 irregularly retouched flakes
1 irregularly retouched blade

MN 399

UTM coordinates: 757020 East / 3516096 North = 35° 42'47.968" East / 31° 45'5.230" North. Altitude above sea level: 346 metres.

5 pieces of flint from a terrace overhanging the northern brink of Wadi Kanisah. Part of the ter-race had clearly fallen down into the floor of the wadi:

2 naviform cores
3 flakes

MN 425

UTM coordinates: 756296 East / 3516036 North = 35° 42'20.423" East / 31° 45'3.870" North. Altitude above sea level: 305 metres.

2 pieces of flint picked up at the southern edge of Wadi Kanisah from a small site destroyed by recent building activities (*Fig. 15*):

1 tang of an arrowhead
1 fragmentary naviform core

MN 465

UTM coordinates: 756707 East / 3520249 North = 35° 42'40.016" East / 31° 47'20.220" North. Altitude above sea level: 174 metres.

29 pieces of pinkish flint from a terrace on the northern side of Wadi 'Uyun Musa. The site was partly cut by the wadi and many flints were found secondarily deposited along the southern slopes of the terrace:

1 end-of-blade scraper
1 borer made on a flake
3 small cores with one platform
1 naviform blade core
1 core fragment
2 secondary crestblades
2 retouched flakes
13 blades, some of them retouched
5 microblades

MN 500

UTM coordinates: 758847 East / 3517976 North = 35° 43'59.129" East / 31° 46'4.734" North. Altitude above sea level: 637 metres.

20 pieces of pinkish flint from a hill south-west of 'Uyun Musa:

1 fragment of an arrowhead with lamellar retouch on the obverse
1 end-of-blade scraper
2 scrapers made on flakes
2 borers made on flakes
1 notched blade
2 backed blades/knives
1 small naviform core
3 core fragments
1 primary core tablet
6 blades

MN 536

UTM coordinates: 758721 East / 3520916 North = 35° 43'57.151" East / 31° 47'40.218" North. Altitude above sea level: 475 metres.

22 pieces of reddish-brown flint picked up from a terrace north-east of Wadi 'Uyun Musa. The collection also comprised 9 pieces of Middle Palaeolithic flint with a yellowish white patina (see above p. 70):

1 fragment of an arrowhead with lamellar retouch on the obverse
1 end-scraper on a blade
2 scrapers made on flakes
2 borers made on flakes

1 notched blade
2 backed blades, one of them with an oblique truncation
5 fragments of naviform cores
1 primary core tablet
7 blades

MN 574

UTM coordinates: 754310 East / 3221145 North = 35° 36'46.285" East / 31° 5'35.9376" North. Altitude above sea level: c. 60 metres.

6 pieces of light pinkish flint picked up from a narrow terrace facing the south-western outlet of Wadi 'Uyun Musa (*Fig. 71*). An additional collection of 52 Upper– Epipalaeolithic artefacts were recovered from the site (see above p. 94):

2 naviform blade cores
3 secondary crest blades
1 backed blade/knife, made on a piece of tabular flint

MN 598

UTM coordinates: 756366 East / 3516571 North = 35° 42'23.286" East / 31° 45'21.171" North. Altitude above sea level: 370 metres.

A collection of 22 light grey to pinkish flints from a hilltop above the northern side of Wadi Kanisah, found around the remains of a circular tomb (**MN 597**):

2 small flake cores with one platform
1 naviform blade core
1 fragment of a naviform blade core
2 secondary crest blades
14 irregularly retouched flakes
2 blades

POTTERY NEOLITHIC CONCENTRATIONS OF FINDS

MN 329

UTM coordinates: 756467 East / 3116315 North = 35° 42'27.179" East / 31° 45'12.784" North. Altitude above sea level: 318 metres.

A collection of 29 sherds, 162 pieces of flint, and 1 piece of ground stone from a low tell north of Wadi

Kanisah, less than 1 metre high and possibly covering an area of c. 30 x 40 metres (*Figs. 91-92*). The northern part of the surface was partly covered by a grey, ashy layer:

29 sherds of strawtempered buff ware, including one sherd with incised herring-bone decoration (*Fig. 93 a*), 1 sherd with plastic decoration (*Fig. 93 c*), 1 sherd of a flat base, 3 sherds with remains of a red wash or slip on the inside, and 1 sherd with traces of a cream-painted decoration on a dark red slip (*Fig. 93 b*).
4 fragmentary arrowheads (*Fig. 93 d-f*)
22 flake scrapers
3 end-of-blade scrapers (*Fig. 93 l*)
4 borers (*Fig. 93 g-i*)
3 awls (*Fig. 93 j-k*)
4 notched blades
2 burins (*Fig. 93 n-o*)
6 sickleblades (*Fig. 93 p*)
1 fragmentary knife (*Fig. 93 m*)
2 heavy points made on cores (*Fig. 94 a-b*)
1 small chipped and polished axe head (*Fig. 94 h*)
3 rough choppers made on cores
6 small flake nodules
26 small blade- and flake cores with on platform (*Fig. 94 c-d*)
1 primary core tablet
3o flakes, some with irregular retouch
40 blades (*Fig. 94 e-g*), some with irregular retouch (*Fig. 93 q-r*)
4 microblades
1 hoe, roughly made from ground stone (*Fig. 94 i*)

MN 423

UTM coordinates: 754704 East / 3520442 North = 35° 41'24.115" East / 31° 47'28.102" North. Altitude above sea level: 130 metres.

A collection of 18 sherds, 50 pieces of flint, and 1 piece of basalt from a plateau (a low tell ?) south of Wadi Kanisah, opposite **MN 329**. The site was covered by bushes and shrub (*Fig. 95*) for which reason its extension could only be approximately determined (c. 50 x 50 metres):

18 sherds of strawtempered buff ware, with slight inclusions of lime particles (*Fig. 96 i-p*), including one sherd with plastic decoration (*Fig. 96 i*), one sherd with red painted decoration on a cream slip (*Fig. 96 j*), and one sherd with incised herring-bone decoration above red-painted bands (*Fig. 96 m*).
1 arrowhead (*Fig. 96 a*)
1 fragmentary arrowhead (*Fig. 96 b*)
1 nosed scraper on a flake
1 burin on a flake (*Fig. 96 c*)
6 segments of sickleblades (*Fig. 96 e-h*)
1 chipped and polished axe head (*Fig. 96 d*)
4 flake cores
3 blade cores
9 core fragments
1 primary core tablet
10 flakes, six of which with irregular retouch
12 blades, half of which with slight retouch
1 fragment of a pestle made of basalt

POTTERY NEOLITHIC SCATTER OF FINDS

MN 526

UTM coordinates: 758930 east / 3529280 North = 35° 44'13.099" East / 31° 52'11.5716" North. Altitude above sea level: 420 metres.

A collection of 11 sherds and 27 flints from what may possibly have been a low tell, north of 'Uyun Musa and next to the Byzantine church of Kayanos (**MN 91**). The site is now destroyed by ploughing and agricultural activities:

11 sherds of strawtempered buff ware with inclusions of lime particles. 1 rimsherd had remains of a red slip or wash inside and outside.
1 end-of-blade scraper
1 burin made on a flake
4 flake- and blade cores
3 fragmentary cores
13 flakes
5 blades

❱ FIG. 80 View towards north showing the Pre-Pottery Neolithic site **MN 417** in the garden on the right bank of Wadi Kanisah. September 1994.

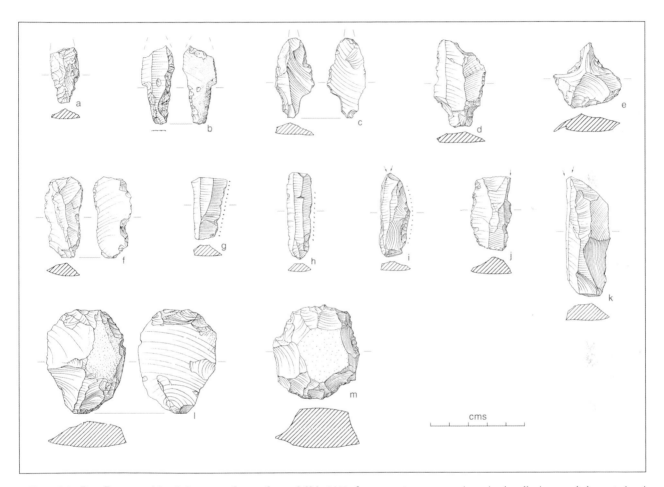

❯ FIG. 81 Pre-Pottery Neolithic artefacts from **MN 417**: fragmentary arrowheads (**a-d**), borer (**e**), notched blade (**f**), sickle blades (**g-h**), burin/sickle blade (**i**), burins (**j-k**), and scrapers (**l-m**).

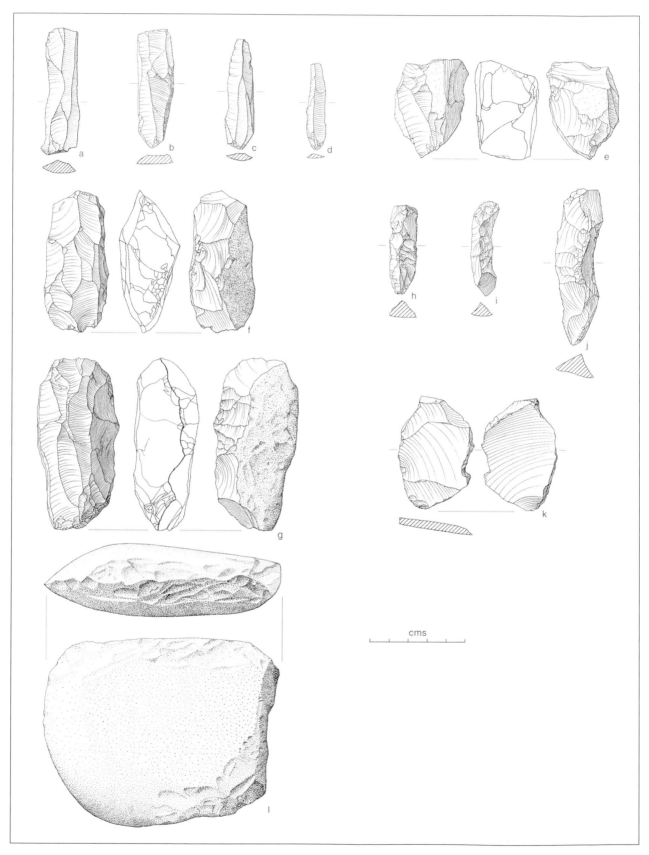

❭ Fig. 82 Pre-Pottery Neolithic artefacts from **MN 417**: blades (**a-d**), naviform blade-and flake cores, (**e-g**), primary crest blades (**h-i**), seconday crest blade (**j**), primary core tablet (**k**), and a large axe of polished stone (**l**).

❯ FIG. 83 View showing the Pre-Pottery Neolithic site **MN 524** situated on the northern side of Wadi Musa in the garden around the house in the middle of the picture. September 1995.

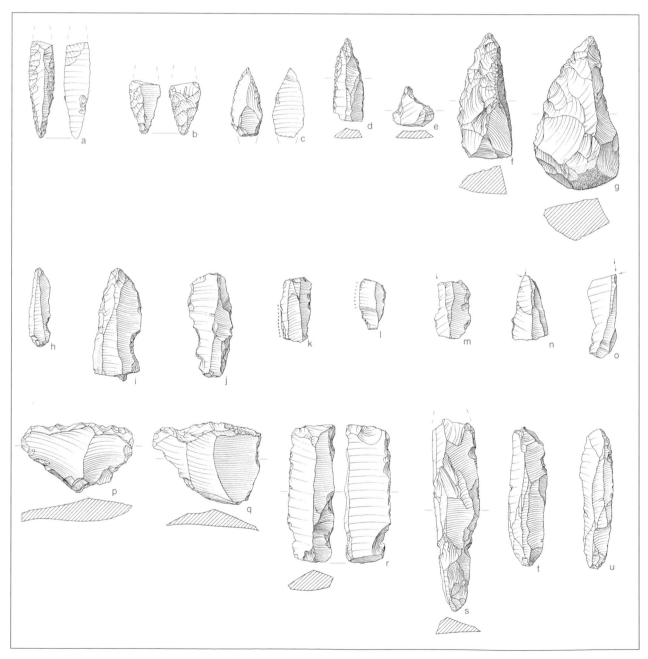

❱ Fɪɢ. 84 Pre-Pottery Neolithic artefacts from **MN 524**: fragmentary arrowheads (**a-c**), borers (**d-e**), picks (**f-g**), notched blades (**h-j**), sickle blades (**k-l**), burins (**m-o**), scrapers (**p-q**), truncated knife (**r**), tanged blade (**s**), and blades (**t-u**).

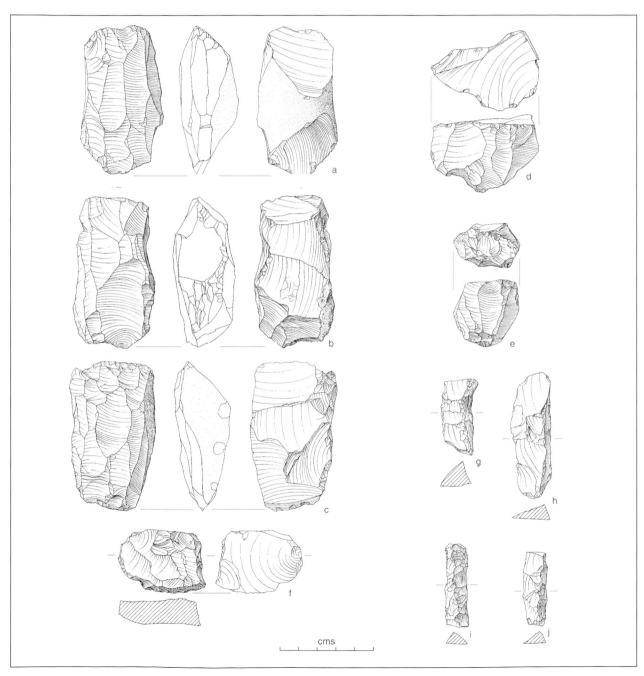

▶ Fɪɢ. 85 Pre-Pottery Neolithic artefacts from **MN 524**: naviform blade- and flake cores (**a-c**), blade- and flake cores with one striking platform (**d-e**), primary core tablet (**f**), and a primary crest blades (**g-j**).

❱ FIG. 86 View towards south-east, across Pre-Pottery Neolithic site **MN 673**. September 1997.

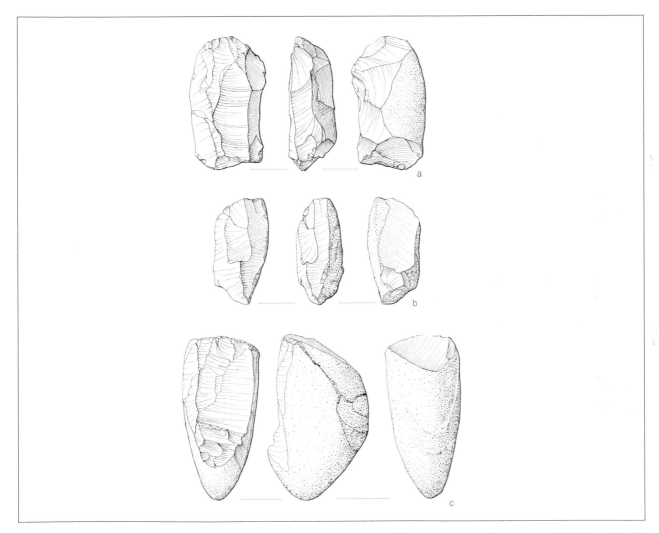

▶ FIG. 87 Pre-Pottery Neolithic artefacts from site **MN 673**: naviform blade- and flake cores (**a-b**), and half-prepared blade core (**c**).

❭ Fɪɢ. 88 View towards south-east across the Pre-Pottery Neolithic site **MN 674**. September 1998.

❯ FIG. 89 Natural outcrop of pinkish flint at the Pre-Pottery Neolithic site **MN 674**. September 1998.

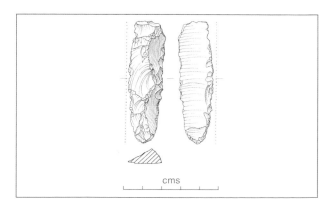

cms

❯ FIG. 90 From **MN 99**. Pre-Pottery Neolithic sickle-blade made on a primary crest blade.

❯ Fɪɢ. 91 View towards east across the Pottery Neolithic site **MN 329**. September 1993.

❱ Fɪɢ. 92 View towards **MN 329**, 15 years later: in the meantime the site has been enclosed by a fence of cactuses and a low wall of stones. September 2008.

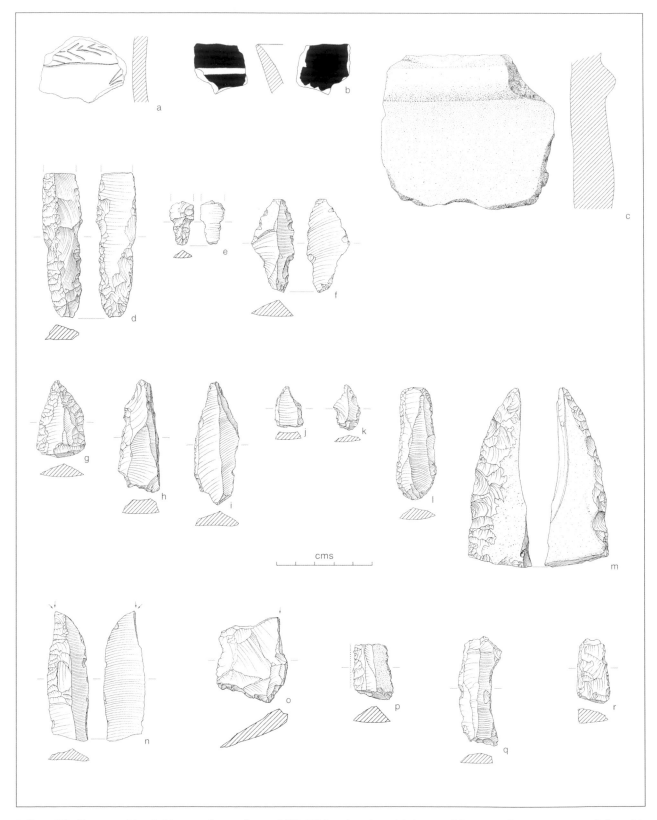

❱ Fig. 93 Pottery Neolithic artefacts from **MN 329**: sherds with incised herring-bone pattern (**a**), with cream painted decoration on a dark red slip (**b**), and with plastic decoration (**c**), fragmentary arrowheads (**d-f**), borers and awls (**g-k**), end-of-blade scraper (**l**) fragmentary knife (**m**), burins (**n-o**), sickle segment (**p**), and retouched blades (**q-r**).

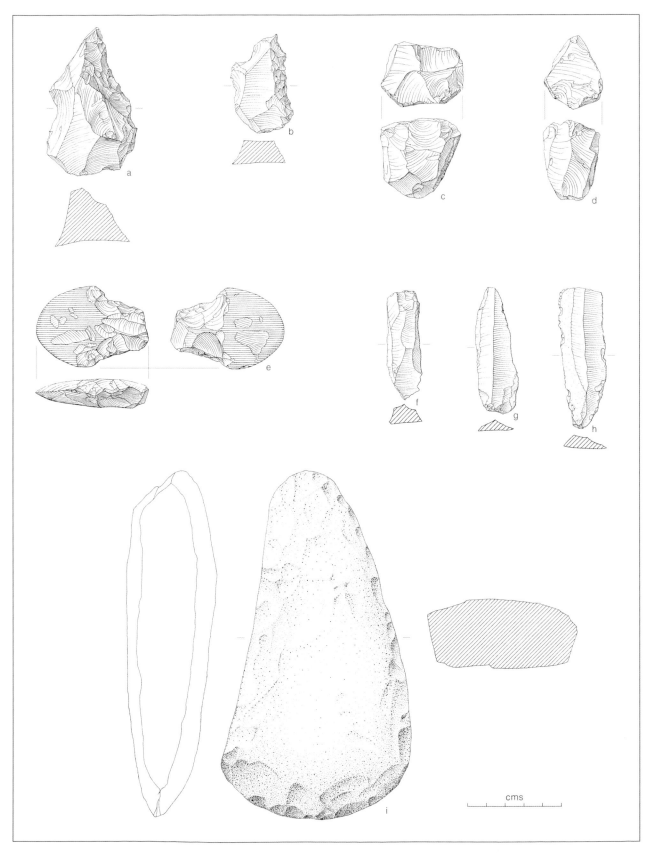

⟩ FIG. 94 Pottery Neolithic artefacts from **MN 329**: heavy points made on cores (**a-b**), flake- and blade cores (**c-d**), small chipped and polished axe head (**e**), blades (**f-h**) and a large hoe of basalt (**i**).

❱ FIG. 95 View towards south across Wadi Kanisah with the Pottery Neolithic site **MN 423** in front of the house in the center of the picture. In the foreground, in the field below the rocks, just opposite **MN 423** on the northern side of Wadi Kanisah, part of the other Pottery Neolithic site **MN 329** is visible. September 1994.

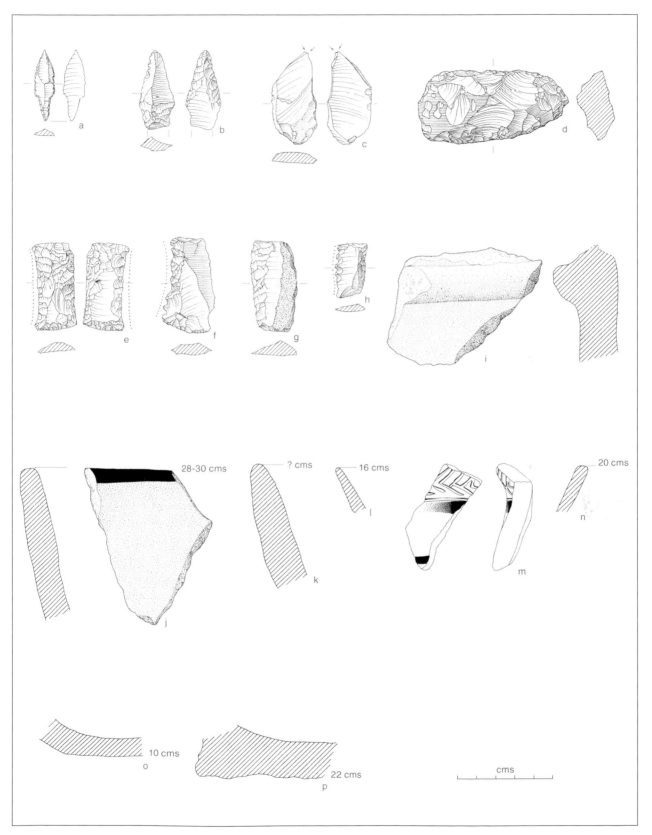

) Fig. 96 Pottery Neolithic artefacts from **MN 423**: arrowheads (**a-b**), burin (**c**), chipped and polished axe head (**d**), sickle segments (**e-h**), sherds of buff ware (**i-p**) one with plastic decoration (**i**), one with red painted decoration on a cream slip (**j**), and one with incised herring-bone decoration above red-painted bands (**m**).

) CONCLUSION (

The archaeological survey of Mount Nebo was carried out during six seasons between 1992 and 1998, followed by a brief reconnaissance in 2008. Centered around Siyagha, the survey covered an area of approximately 35 square kilometres with the two major valleys Wadi 'Uyun Musa and Wadi Jadidah/Wadi Kanisah as the most important topographical features.

The main purpose of the survey was first of all to locate, describe, register and map the archaeological sites and monuments in the region, so that the most important sites in the future might be protected from destruction caused by recent building development, road construction, or agricultural activities involving the use of tractors and bulldozers. During the survey 748 sites, monuments, and single finds were registered, spread in time from the Lower Palaeolithic to the Late Ottoman periods. Our attention was primarily concentrated on the large number of megalithic monuments in the area: 194 dolmens, 41 lines of stones and menhirs, and 316 circular megalithic tombs. Together with the finds from later periods they will be described in two successive publications.

The present volume is dedicated to the description of 79 locations and single finds, which can be attributed to the Stone Age. For an understanding of how the collections from these sites were obtained, it may be relevant to repeat that our aim was limited to making a chronological identification of the assemblages and their distribution in the landscape, based on diagnostic artefacts. Therefore we did not, in the field, make any attempt to collect all objects or to make a systematic study of their distribution within the individual site. Using a method by which a limited collection of artefacts were removed from the locations, it should be possible in the future to identify the archaeological sites where enough material has been left to carry out further systematic investigations in case this would seem to be appropriate. It appears that out of the 79 collections we have identified as belonging to the Stone Age, only 25 *concentrations* of artefacts seem to represent an actual occupation of the site. The remainder are small *scatters* of flint or diagnostic *single finds* such as for example handaxes. The distribution by period of the 25 concentrations of artefacts is as follows:

2 Lower Palaeolithic sites: Upper Acheulean (c. 250,000 – 150,000 years bp)
9 Middle Palaeolithic sites: Levallois-Mousterian /Tabun B (c. 70,000 – 47,000 years bp – or later?)
8 Upper– Epipalaeolithic sites: Late Levantine Aurignacien / Early Kebaran (c. 25,000 – 15,000 bp)
4 Pre-Pottery Neolithic sites: Middle PPNB (c. 10,000 – 9,500 bp)
2 Pottery Neolithic sites: Yarmukian and Pottery Neolithic A/ Jericho IX (c. 7,000 – 6,000 bp)

The two Lower Palaeolithic locations are both open-air sites representing one or several occupations, one in an altitude of 746 metres with a fine view across Wadi 'Uyun Musa, the other situated on a high saddle-shaped plateau facing Wadi Hisban, only 40 metres above sea level. The inventory of the sites suggests that they were seasonally occupied by hunters.

Most of the Middle Palaeolithic and Upper– Epipalaeolithic open-air sites in the Mount Nebo area are situated along or near the two wadi systems. During the Pleistocene and Holocene periods the region faced a series of environmental changes and climatic fluctuations. However, in the later part of the Middle Palaeolithic, as well as during the late Upper Palaeolithic, and especially after c. 25,000 years bp, the landscape above the wadies seems to have been dominated by open steppe grassland with a sporadical growth of trees. In this perspective it is tempting to interpret the small concentrations of Levallois-Mousterian artefacts in the Mount Nebo region – as well as the Upper– Epipalaeolithic concentrations – as representing a pattern of transhumance with small seasonal campsites used temporarily by minor groups of hunter-gatherers on the move between winter encampments in the Jordan Rift Valley and the higher and cooler areas on the Jordanian Central Plateau and at the Syrian Steppe. The sites were probably all non-permanent, although they may have been visited continuously year by year during longer periods of time. This might as well be the case with the settlements, which seem to be related to the occupation of five rock-shelters in the Epipalaeolithic period. The first permanent settlement in the region is connected with the earliest evidence of farming. Two low Pre-Pottery Neolithic tells were situated respectively on the right bank of Wadi Kanisah and the right bank of Wadi 'Uyun Musa. Later, two small Pottery Neolithic tells facing each other on either side of Wadi Kanisah may well represent one settlement, just divided by the stream of water in Wadi Kanisah.

Considering the settlement patterns of the Mont Nebo area through time, it is conspicuous that the region was not continuously inhabited through the ages. On the contrary there is a considerable gap between the exploitation of the region by *homo erectus* in the Upper Acheulean period (c. 250,000 – 150,000 years bp) and the arrival of Neanderthals, possibly around 70,000 years bp. Minor gaps, unaccounted for as well, appear between the early Epipalaeolithic/Kebaran sites and the settlements of the Pre-Pottery Neolithic B period, and between these and the early Pottery Neolithic settlement. Most remarkable, however, is the apparent gap between the Middle Palaeolithic (c. 70,000 – 47,000 years bp – or later) and the late Upper– Epipalaeolithic occupation of the Mount Nebo region (c. 25,000 – 15,000 years bp).

In recent years the spread of Modern Humans (*homo sapiens sapiens*) and the gradual extinction of Neanderthals in the Near East have been the subject of much attention. Traditionally, the Neanderthals were associated with the Middle Palaeolithic Levallois-Mousterian tradition and the Modern Humans with the blade traditions characteristic of the Upper Palaeolithic. However, it has been clearly demonstrated that the appearance of the Modern Humans cannot be linked entirely to the technological changes at the transition from the Middle- to the Upper Palaeolithic.[29] Furthermore,

---

[29] Cf. e.g. Potter 1995: 506 and Clark, Coinman and Neeley 2001: 49 ff.

there is now evidence from the Near East that "[…] *Moderns and Neanderthals would have been within the same geographical area for more than 60,000 years.*"[30]

For the time being this might lead to the suggestion that in the Mount Nebo region – as well as in the interior areas of Jordan and Syria – we may have had a longer Mousterian tradition, represented by Neanderthals, and extending beyond the Middle Palaeolithic into the Upper Palaeolithic period. This might explain part of the enigma relating to the scarcity or apparent lack of classical Upper Palaeolithic sites in the Mount Nebo region, where possibly small groups of Neanderthals, superseded by Modern Humans along the Levantine coast, survived and appeared sporadically for several millennia towards the last phase of the Upper Palaeolithic period. In this case the earliest reliable evidence of activities which can be related to the presence of Modern Humans in the area is the Epipalaeolithic finds from the rock-shelters and open-air sites along the wadies of Mount Nebo.

----

[30] Finlayson 2004: 152. According to Finlayson, the last Neanderthal populations on record occur around 31-28,000 years bp. In his opinion "[…] *the extinction of a human population, such as the Neanderthals, in Eurasia during the Pleistocene would not have been a singular event. The ultimate courses […] are probably very similar in all cases. Populations became fragmented and were unable to recover. Climatic acting on habitats and resources were primarily responsible for range conditions and population fragmentation and reduction*" (Finlayson 2004: 150).

) BIBLIOGRAPHY (

Adams, R. B. (ed.) (2008). *Jordan. An Archaeological Reader.* London/Oakville.

Akazawa, T., Aoki, K. and Bar-Yosef, O. (eds.) (1998). *Neanderthals and Modern Humans in Western Asia*. New York and London.

Bar-Yosef, O. (1970). *The Epipalaeolithic Cultures of Palestine.* Ph. D. Thesis, The Hebrew University of Jerusalem.

Bar-Yosef, O., Goldberg, P. and Leveson, T. (1974). Late Quarternary Stratigraphy and Prehistory in Wadi Fazael, Jordan Valley: A Preliminary Report. *Paléorient*, 2,2: 415-428.

Benedettucci, F. (1998). The Iron Age. *In*: Piccirillo, M. and Alliata, E (eds.), 1998: 110-127.

Bintliff, J. (2002). Time, Process and Catastrophism in the Study of Mediterranean Alluvial History: a Review. *World Archaeology*, 33: 417-435.

Bisson, M. S. *et al.* (2007). Neanderthals at the Crossroads. Middle Palaeolithic Sites on the Madaba Plateau, Jordan. *In*: Levy, T. E. *et al.* (eds.) 2007: 179-186.

Bossut, P., Kafafi, Z. and G. Dollfus (1988). Khirbet ed-Dharih (Survey Site 49/WHS 524), un nouveau gisement néolithique avec céramique du Sud-Jordanien. *Paléorient*, 14,1: 127-131.

Butzer, K. W. (2005). Environmental History in the Mediterranean World. *Journal of Archaeological Science*, 32: 1773-1800.

Chazan, M. (2001). Bladelet Production in the Aurignacien of Hayonim Cave, Israel. *Paléorient*, 27,1: 81-88.

Clark, G. A., Coinman, N. R. and Neeley, M. P. (2001). The Palaeolithic of Jordan in a Levantine Context. *Studies in the History and Archaeology of Jordan,* VII: 49-77.

Coinman, N. R. (2002). New Evidence of Ksar Akil Scrapers in the Levantine Upper Paleolithic. *Paléorient*, 28,2: 87-104.

Coinman, N. R. and Olszewski, D.I. (2007). Midnight at the Oasis. The End of the Pleistocene in Wadi al-Hasa. *In*: Levy, T. E. *et al.* (eds.) 2007: 187-194.

Conder, C. R. (1885). *Heth and Moab. Explorations in Syria in 1881 and 1882.* London.

Conder, C. R. (1889). *The Survey of Eastern Palestine*. London.

De Saulcy, F. (1865). *Voyage en Terre Sainte*, I-II. Paris.

Finlayson, C. (2004). *Neanderthals and Modern Humans. An Ecological and Evolutionary Perspective.* Cambridge.

Folsach, K. von, Thrane, H. and Thuesen, I. (eds.) (2004). *From Handaxe to Khan. Essays Presented to Peder Mortensen on the Occasion of his 70th Birthday.* Aarhus.

Gebel, H. G. and Kozlowski, S. K. (eds.) (1994). *Neolithic Chipped Stone Industries of the Fertile Crescent.* Studies in Early Near Eastern Production, Subsistence, and Environment, 1. Berlin.

Garrard, A. N. and Byrd, B.F. (1992). New Dimensions to the Epipalaeolithic of the Wadi El-Jilat in Central Jordan. *Paléorient*, 18,1: 47-62.

Garrod, D. A. E. (1954). Excavations at the Mugharet Kebara, Mount Carmel, 1931: The Aurignacian Industries. *Proceedings of the Prehistoric Society*, XX,2: 155-192.

Henley, E., Cambell, S. and Maeda, O. (eds.) (2011). *The State of the Stone: Terminologies, Continuities and Contexts in the Near Eastern Lithics.* (Studies in Early Near Eastern Production, Subsistence, and Environment, 13). Berlin, *ex oriente*.

Henry, D. O. (2007). Searching for Neanderthals and Finding Ourselves. Research at Tor Faraj. *In*: Levi T. E. *et al.* (eds.) 2007: 171-177.

Kenyon, K. and Holland, T. A. (1982). *Excavations at Jericho IV. The Pottery Type Series and other Finds*. London.

Levy, T. E. *et al.* (eds.) (2007). *Crossing Jordan. North American Contributions to the Archaeology of Jordan.* London / Oakville.

Luynes, Le Duc de (1874). *Voyage d'exploration à la Mer Morte à Petra et sur la rive gauche du Jourdain,* I. Paris.

Macumber, P. G. (2008). Evolving Landscape and Environment of Jordan. *In*: Adams, R. B. (ed.), 2008: 7-34.

Maher, L. *et al.* (2001). Middle Epipalaeolithic Sites in Wadi Ziqlab, Northern Jordan. *Paléorient*, 27,1: 5-19.

Maher, L. A. and Richter, T. (2011). PPN Predecessors: Current Issues in Late Pleistocene Chipped Stone Analyses in the Southern Levant. In: Healey, E., Cambell, S. and Maeda, O. (eds.), 2011: 25-31.

Mortensen, P. (1970). A Preliminary Study of the Chipped Stone Industry from Beidha. *Acta Archaeologica*, 41: 1-54.
– (1992). A Survey in the Mount Nebo Area 1992. *Studium Biblicum Franciscanum, Liber Annuus,* XLII. Jerusalem: 344-346.

– (1993). Paleolithic and Epipaleolithic Sites in the Hulailan Valley, Northern Luristan. *In*: Olszewski, D. I. and Dibble, H. L. (eds.), *The Paleolithic Prehistory of the Zagros-Taurus*. (University Museum Monograph 83), University of Pennsylvania 1993: 159-186.

– (1996). Mount Nebo Survey. *American Journal of Archaeology*, 100,3: 511.

– (2002). Archaeological Excavations at "Conder's Circle" at 'Ayn Jadidah near Mount Nebo. *Studium Biblicum Franciscanum, Liber Annuus*, LII. Jerusalem: 471-472.

– (2005). Archaeological Investigations at "Conder's Circle" at 'Ayn Jadidah near Mount Nebo. *Studium Biblicum Franciscanum, Liber Annuus*, LV. Jerusalem: 485.

– (2009). New Light on the Palaeolithic Landscape around Mount Nebo. *Studies in the History and Archaeology of Jordan*, X: 917-920.

Mortensen, P. and Thuesen, I. (1998). The Prehistoric Periods. *In*: Piccirillo, M. and Alliata, E. (eds.), 1998: 84-99.

– (2007). Investigating "Conder's Circle" at 'Ayn Jadida, near Mount Nebo. *Studies in the History and Archaeology of Jordan*, IX: 451-456.

Muhesen, S. (2004). An Introduction to the Palaeolithic of Syria. *In*: Folsach K. von, Thrane, H. and Thuesen, I (eds.), 2004: 29-48.

al-Nahar, M. and Clark, G. A. (2009). The Lower Palaeolithic in Jordan. *Jordan Journal for History and Archaeology*, 3,2: 173-215.

Neeley, M. P. (2010). TBAS 106: A Late Natufian Site in West-Central Jordan. *Neo-Lithics*, 1/10: 86-91.

Olszewski, D. I. (2006). Issues in the Levantine Epipalaeolithic: The Madamaghan, Nebekian and Qalkhan (Levant Epipalaeolithic). *Paléorient*, 32,1: 19-26.

– (2008). The Palaeolithic Period, including the Epipalaeolithic. *In*: Adams, R. B. (ed.), 2008: 35-69.

Palumbo, G. (1994). *The Jordan Antiquities Database and Information System (JADIS). A Summary of the Data*. Amman.

– (1998). The Bronze Age. *In*: Piccirillo, M. and Alliata, E. (eds.), 1998: 100-109.

Piccirillo, M. (1991). Mosaikkerne i Jordan. *In*: *2000 års Farvepragt. Dragter og Mosaikker fra Palæstina og Jordan. Moesgård Museum, Århus*: 30-63.

– (1998). The Exploration of Mount Nebo. *In*: Piccirillo, M. and Alliata, E. (eds.), 1998: 13-51.

Piccirillo, M. and Alliata, E. (eds), (1998). *Mount Nebo. New Excavations 1967-1997*. (Studium Biblicum Franciscanum Collectio Maior 27). Jerusalem.

Piccirillo, M. and Palumbo, G. (1993). Proposal for the Zoning of the Mount Nebo Archaeological Park. *Studium Biblicum Franciscanum, Liber Annuus*, XLII. Jerusalem: 463-466.

Potter, J. M. (1995). Lithic Technology and Settlement Pattern Variability within the Levantine Mousterian: A Comparison of Sites WHS 621 and WHS 634 from Wadi al-Hasa. *Studies in the History and Archaeology of Jordan*, IX: 157-166.

Quintero, L. A., Wilke, P. J. and Rollefson, G. (2004 a). The Eastern Levant, the Pleistocene, and Palaeoanthropology. *ACOR Newsletter,* 16,1: 1-3.
– (2004 b). An Eastern Jordan Perspective on the Lower Palaeolithic of the "Levantine Corridor". *Studies in the History and Archaeology of Jordan,* IX: 157-166.

Richter, T. (2011). Nebekian, Qalkhan and Kebaran: Variability, Classification and Interaction. New Insights from the Azraq Oases. *In*: Healey, E., Cambell, S. and Maeda, O. (eds.), 2011: 33-49.

Richter, D. *et al.* (2001). The Middle to Upper Palaeolithic Transition in the Levant and New Thermoluminescence Dates for a Late Mousterian Assemblage from Jefr Al-Ajla (Syria). *Paléorient,* 27,2: 29-46.

Ripamonti, J. A. (1963). *Investigationes sobre la tomba de Moises.* Caracas.

Rollefson, G. (2008). The Neolithic Period. *In*: Adams, R. B. (ed.), 2008: 71-108.

Sabelli, R. and Dinelli, O. (1998). The Region of Nebo. An Area to be Protected. *In*: Piccirillo, M. and Alliata, E. (eds.), 1998: 604-608.

Saller, S. J. (1941). *The Memorial of Moses on Mount Nebo,* I-II: Text & Plates. (Studium Biblicum Franciscanum Collectio Maior 1). Jerusalem.
– (1966). Iron Age Tombs at Nebo, Jordan. *Studium Biblicum Franciscanum Liber Annuus,* XVI. Jerusalem: 165-298.

Saller, S. J. and Bagatti, B. (1949). *The Town of Nebo (Khirbet el-Mekhayyat).* (Studium Biblicum Franciscanum Collectio Maior 7). Jerusalem.

Schneider, H. (1950). *The Memorial of Moses at Mount Nebo,* III: The Pottery. (Studium Biblicum Franciscanum. Collectio Maior 1). Jerusalem.

Stockton, E. (1967). Stone Age Culture in the Nebo Region. *Studium Biblicum Franciscanum Liber Annuus,* XVII. Jerusalem: 122-128.

Thuesen, I. (2004). Messages in Stone. The Megaliths of the Nebo Region in Jordan. *In*: Follsach K. von, Thrane, H., and Thuesen, I. (eds.), 2004: 105-117.
– (2009). From Jericho to Mount Nebo: Results of Recent Excavations of Conder's Circle. *Studies in the History and Archaeology of Jordan,* X: 603-609.

Walmsley, A. (2007). *Early Islamic Syria. An Archaeological Assessment.* London.